P-51: bomber escort

P-51: bomber escort

William Hess

Editor-in-Chief: Barrie Pitt
Editor: David Mason
Art Director: Sarah Kingham
Picture Editor: Robert Hunt
Consultant Art Editor: Denis Piper
Designer: David A Evans
Illustration: John Batchelor
Photographic Research: Johnathan Moore
Cartographer: Richard Natkiel

Photographs for this book were especially selected from the following Archives: from left to right pages 4-10
US Air Force; 11 North American Rockwell; 11-13 USAF; 14-16 NA Rockwell; 16 WN Hess Collection; 18-19 WN
Hess; 20-21 USAF; 22 WN Hess; 23 USAF; 24-25 WN Hess; 27 Imperial War Museum; 28-29 US Army; 30-31 USAF
33 IWM; 33 WN Hess; 35 USAF; 35 IWM; 36 US Signal Corps; 37-45 USAF; 48-50 NA Rockwell; 52-54 USAF; 56
WN Hess; 57-87 USAF; 88-91 NA Rockwell; 93 WN Hess; 94 Dr Alexander Bernfes; 96 USAF; 97 William Green;
98 USAF; 100-101 WN Hess; 102-105 USAF; 106 US National Archives; 108-131 USAF; 132-133 WN Hess; 134-138
USAF; 139 WN Hess; 140-149 USAF; 150-151 NA Rockwell; 152-159 USAF; Front cover: USAF; Back cover:
USAF

SBN 345-24724-8-200

First Printing: December, 1971
Second Printing: April, 1975

Printed in the United States of America

BALLANTINE BOOKS
A Division of Random House, Inc.
201 East 50th Street, New York, N.Y. 10022

Contents

Prologue

On the historic day of 4th March 1944 a khaki-colored Ford sedan pulled up to a hard-stand on Debden Aerodrome, England, where a P-51 Mustang stood glistening in the gloomy and dark early morning air. An American officer got out of the automobile and strode over to the aircraft where he was greeted by Sargeant Harry East, the Chief of his ground crew.

Colonel Don Blakeslee mounted the wing and then proceeded to fit himself into the crowded cockpit of the Mustang whose fuselage sides were marked with the blue and white national insignia flanked by large black letters, WD-C. The battery cart was plugged in and moments later the big four-bladed propeller began to

turn. The engine caught with a staccato bark and slowly the Mustang began to move down the taxiway where it would precede a long line of red-nosed aircraft. The ground crew and station personnel peered enviousy after them. Today Colonel Blakeslee was leading the 4th Fighter Group to escort the bombers of the Eighth Air Force to that long-awaited target – Berlin.

Forty-eight Mustangs set course across the Channel and headed for the rendezvous where they were to take over escort duty from the P-47 Thunderbolts whose range would not permit them to go all the way with the bombers. The further the fighters went the worse the weather became, and as

mediately Blakeslee got onto the tail of a 109 and lined up to give fire. He pressed the gun button, but nothing happened. The guns were frozen. Although he was the first Mustang pilot over Berlin, aerial victory was not to be his that day. Pushing his throttle to the firewall he drew up alongside the Messerschmitt and gave him a disgusted wave. The German pilot waggled his wings and broke off in a long dive into the clouds.

However, other Mustang pilots were to see Berlin and down German aircraft that day. Lieutenant Charles Anderson went down and got a look at the city through a small hole in the clouds, but was immediately jumped by six Focke-Wulf 190s. He quickly took cover in the clouds, waited for a few moments and then popped out. The 190s were still there, so he plunged back into the clouds and set course for home.

Captain Nicholas 'Cowboy' Megura chased a German fighter to the deck and found himself over an aerodrome on the outskirts of Berlin. He sighted a Junkers Ju 52 transport on the field, gave it a short burst and saw it go up in flames. Then he, too, headed for home. Lieutenant Paul S Riley got on the tail of a German fighter, fired, and the German went into a dive. As they both dived down toward the ground Riley's windshield promptly frosted up and he broke off and pulled up.

Blakeslee assembled his scattered fighters and headed them back toward England. It had not been a spectacular mission or even a productive one for the Mustang pilots, but their mere presence over the capital of the Third Reich had its significance. After the end of the Second World War the defeated Reich Marshal Hermann Göring made a statement to the press concerning the presence of escort fighters: 'The first time your bombers came over Hanover escorted by fighters, I began to be worried. When they came with fighter escort over Berlin – I knew the jig was up.'

they struggled higher and higher to get above the solid cloud cover many were forced to turn back owing to mechanical troubles and oxygen shortages.

Shortly after noon the B-17 Flying Fortresses were sighted. Blakeslee and his Mustangs took up their positions forward and above the bomber stream in order to ward off any German fighters which might come up to challenge. Just as the B-17s let go their bombs the specks that would grow into German fighters began to appear on the horizon.

Blakeslee and his flight sighted some fifteen Messerschmitt 109s and Focke-Wulf 190s headed for the bombers and dived down into them. Im-

Birth of the Mustang

September 1939 saw Hitler's armies invade and crush Poland in the first of the *blitzkreig* campaigns. With the conquest of that small country complete, Hitler turned his attention to the west where the armies of France and Britain took up station behind the reputedly impregnable Maginot Line.

During the conquest of Poland, the German Luftwaffe had gained immediate fame. The performance of the Messerschmitt 109 fighter, the Junkers Ju 87 'Stuka' dive bomber and the Heinkel He 111 had dominated the headlines during those weeks. Their terror from the skies campaign struck fear into the hearts and minds of the Allied nations of Europe.

The Royal Air Force possessed several squadrons of Hawker Hurricanes and Supermarine Spitfires, but not in sufficient numbers to meet requirements over an extended period of time. France had already contracted a number of Curtiss Hawk 75 fighters from the United States and was doing its best to get more. As the Purchasing Commissions from these two nations visited the United States in the winter 1939-40 the stage was set for the creation and birth of the North American P-51 Mustang.

The British had contracted for several hundred Curtiss P-40 type aircraft and in order to increase production of the craft it had been suggested that they might try to get the young North American Aviation Company to equip themselves for production of the fighter plane. With this in mind the British sent representatives of their Air Purchasing Commission to see James H 'Dutch' Kindelberger, President of North American Aviation, to attempt to contract his company to build the Curtiss design for them.

Kindelberger was a man of foresight who had closely followed the development of military aircraft in Europe and he had realised early in the war

The sleek and purposeful nose of a Merlin-engined Mustang

Kindelberger sold the Mustang to the British when it was no more than an idea; the order for several hundred P-40s was cancelled

that the fighter aircraft designs that were being built in the United States were not going to be able to cope with the new German fighters that were already in action.

When the British Purchasing Commission presented their plan to Kindelberger in April 1940 he turned it down. He felt that the engineering team he possessed could come up with a brand new fighter plane that would outperform the P-40. Kindelberger informed the commission that he could build a new fighter and put it into production in the same length of time that it would take to tool up to manufacture the Curtiss fighter. Lee Atwood, Vice-President of North American, laid out the proposal for the new aircraft before the British representatives. The original drawings were

those of Raymond H Rice, chief engineer, and the designer was Edgar Schmued.

The aircraft design, designated NA-73 by North American, was to be made up in many parts incorporating features that would lend themselves to mass production. The design would also utilise new features that would make the plane an outstanding performer in the air. The promise which really persuaded the British was that North American could produce prototype model of the aircraft in 120 days. After due deliberation, the British representatives accepted the design with the 120-day stipulation and designated the design 'Mustang'.

Immediately Kindelberger and Atwood returned to the plant in Inglewood, California, and got the structural design group to work on the project. As quickly as preliminary studies and data were completed, the findings were air mailed to the British Commission in New York. Kindelberg-

er got the final go-ahead to build the aircraft three weeks after his return to California.

Usual routine red tape and office orders were forgotten. Communication was via inter-office memo or by word of mouth A full size mockup of the aircraft was begun and as soon as data was available it was rushed to the cabinetmakers there. A $20,000 mahogany one-quarter scale model of the design was also carved out by the wind tunnel group.

The basic design called for the use of an in-line engine in order to come up with a smooth nose and a frontal area of minimum drag. To utilise this design it was immediately obvious that the only American manufactured engine which would fit the bill would be the Allison V-1710, 12-cylinder, liquid-cooled power plant.

An aerodynamic duct or scoop was designed to be located under the fuselage to facilitate ram air for the coolant radiator located aft of the cockpit

Above: 'Dutch' Kindelberger with his protégé. *Below:* The P-51's designer, Edgar Schmued

in the fuselage. This not only utilised a bit of thrust as derived from the ram air to eject the warmed airflow, but also cut down further the drag factor.

A new inovation incorporated into the design was that of the laminar flow or low drag airfoil. Whereas conventional airfoils tended to build up turbulence when their frontal area was subjected to shock waves, the laminar flow wing's greatest thickness was moved well back where it was followed by a teardrop-shaped trailing edge. This caused air to flow more smoothly up the longer incline of the leading edge to the point of greatest thickness before breaking down into the turbulent flow area which increased drag. This spread out the pressure producing the wing lift.

The contours of the laminar flow wing permitted the air to build up desired pressures over double the area of more conventional wings. The shock waves were thus reduced and increased speed and smoothness were attained. The laminar flow wing was at that time unproven and it was agreed that if this wing did not perform up to expectation within thirty days a conventional wing would be substituted.

When the mahogany model was put into the wind tunnel for testing at the California Institute of Technology it was feared that the new wing was going to be inadequate. Although the drag was the lowest on record during the test, stalling characteristics were bad. The model was modified and put back into the tunnel for testing a week later and again the little silk tufts glued to the wing surfaces failed to act satisfactorily. North American engineers then began to suspect that the wind tunnel was not large enough for satisfactory testing. The wing was loaded into an airplane and flown to a larger wind tunnel at the University of Washington in Seattle

Air scoop under the Mustang's fuselage to facilitate ram air for the coolant radiator

NA-73X, the original prototype, delights the pilots with its excellent performance

where it passed its tests with flying colors.

Some modification was required of the radiator air scoop where turbulence was being built up in wind tunnel tests. This was eliminated by dropping the entrance lip of the scoop a mere one inch. The disc brake assemblies called for in the original design were not available at the time and a temporary installation was made by using the wheels from an AT-6, advanced training aircraft.

Armament was to British specification. The initial production models would mount two .30 caliber machine guns under the engine cowling to fire through the propeller. Outboard in each wing were mounted two .50 caliber machine guns.

Slowly, the prototype took shape and by October the installation of the Allison engine had begun. This was

completed in four days and on 11th October, 1940, the first Mustang was rolled out into the sunlight. For two weeks ground tests were performed and controls were adjusted. These were highly satisfactory· and on the morning of 26th October, 1940, test pilot Vance Breese climbed into the cockpit for the initial test flight.

Breese taxied out to the end of the runway and put the craft through its checks. All went well so he positioned the plane in the center of the runway and pushed the throttle forward. As he raced along his initial finding was that the problem of torque was not nearly as great as had been anticipated. A little rudder easily compensated for this and the tail rose shortly after the roll started. The first Mustang was airborne.

Breese proceeded to put the aircraft through its paces and its performance far exceeded initial expectations. It maneuvered ably and handled beautifully. After twenty minutes Breese brought the Mustang in for a smooth landing at Mines Field.

Further flights went well as the Mustang showed that it was a superior fighter plane and all the engineering team at North American revelled in its performance. The only misfortune in the testing program took place on the air-speed calibration flight on the morning of 20th November. The aircraft was airborne at 7 am with test pilot Paul Balfour at the controls. As he began to make his calibration passes at 250 feet the Allison engine coughed and then cut out. Balfour could not make a return to the field at his low altitude so he was forced to attempt a landing in a rough field. The Mustang slipped in easily but on hitting the soft ground the nose went up and the craft flipped over on its back. The original Mustang, NA-73X, was a write-off, but the pilot was uninjured. There had been no aerodynamic failure, the plane had run out of fuel on the selected tank.

The outstanding performance of the original Mustang brought an order of 320 aircraft by the RAF. This order was permitted by the United States with the agreement that the fifth and tenth production models would go to the US Army Air Force. These planes were duly delivered to the Army Air Force test facility at Wright Field, Ohio. Regretfully, there they gathered dust and remained virtually unnoticed for many months.

Kindleberger got his production line into high gear and began to get his Mustangs moving. A year later, in November 1941, the first Mustang Mark I, so designated by the RAF, arrived in Liverpool harbor.

The aircraft was taken to Burtonwood for assembly and testing was begun by the end of the month. Machine guns were installed along

Late prototype armed Mustang, the shape of things to come

Above: An RAF Mark I; British observers were initially dubious about the performance figures claimed for their P-51s. *Below:* Messerschmitt Bf 109s; tragedies recurred throughout the war because of the similar profiles of the German fighter and the Mustang

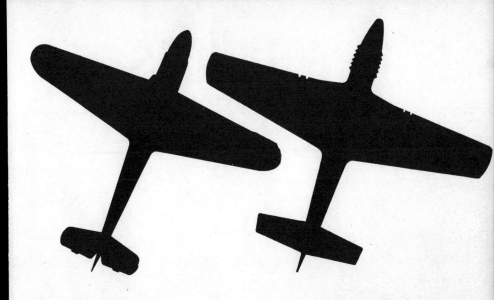

In action, it was often found that pilots tended to confuse the Messerschmitt Bf 109 and the P-51 Mustang. Illustrated here are a Bf 109F and a P-51B. Looking at silhouettes such as these, it is easy to point out the differences; the relatively longer fuselage, rounded wingtips and differently shaped tailplane (with tabs) of the Bf 109 and the squatter appearance and exhaust stubs of the P-51. But in combat, where recognition had to be instantaneous and made after only a fleeting glance at an aircraft approaching possibly out of the sun or through cloud, pilots would more naturally note the more obvious similarities: both were powered by liquid-cooled inline engines, were compact single seaters, had low mounted wings with a straight taper on leading and trailing edges and similar tailplanes. In profile, both had similar fuselages, especially around the cockpit, And national markings would probably only be seen at the last minute, when it would be too late to rectify an earlier fault in recognition.

with communications equipment, and the aircraft was ready to become airborne. An American test pilot put the craft through its initial paces and he reported a level flight speed of 390mph at 14,000 feet. This the British observers tended to doubt until official calculations could be worked out.

During its official tests for the RAF the test pilot brought the Mustang down in a dive at over 500mph and in the course of calibrated level flight airspeed tests it logged 382mph. This seemed to end the doubts of the observers as to just what the Mustang could do in the way of speed.

One particular problem that presented itself at this time was that of recognition. The general lines of the Mustang in flight resembled those of the Messerschmitt 109. Recognition posters had to be prepared as quickly as possible and were sent out to all observer and Royal Air Force stations. As an added precaution each of the production Mustangs coming into the British Isles had a yellow band, one foot in width, painted around the chord of the wing. Regardless of these recognition precautions the profile of the Mustang would present a problem to the end of the war as many a fighter pilot will attest.

However, the engineers at North American had produced a superior fighter, the RAF was quite pleased with their offering and the Mustang was now ready for combat.

Early operations

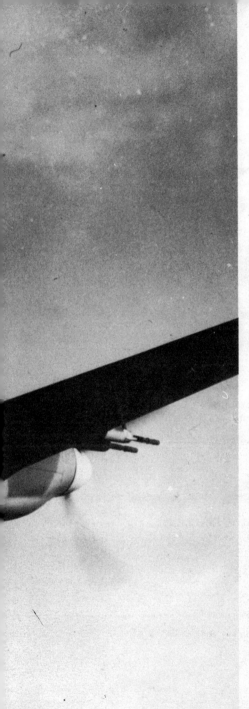

Due to the lack of climb rate and poor high altitude performance of the Allison engine the RAF relegated the new Mustang to duties with the Army Co-operation Command. The pilots and personnel of this unit were members of the RAF, but they were attached to the army for tactical purposes. The operational purpose of aircraft assigned to this command was to destroy enemy communications, transportation, troop movements, barges, light shipping, ammunition and fuel dumps. To accomplish these duties the Mustang was flown at very low altitudes ranging from tree top level to 6,000 feet. There were three primary purposes in maintaining such low levels. First, it made it very difficult for enemy fighters to dive down to attack. Secondly, the lack of altitude and speed of the Mustang made ground fire largely ineffective, and thirdly, it put the aircraft under the detection range of enemy radar.

The speed and sensitive controls of the Mustang made it an excellent aircraft for this type of job. A good example of this work is a description of the ground support mission of two Mustangs during the British commando raid on the port of Dieppe on 19th August, 1942.

The two stubby-winged fighters swooped low over the water and skipped from barge-top to wave-top like flat stones hurled across the water. Salt spray spattered their bellies and wing surfaces as they roared towards the Continent. As they neared land they pulled up to clear the rigging and masts of an offshore fleet of small ships.

Gunfire broke out on the beach, but the Mustangs charged inland, dodging flak and seeking out their check points. Their instructions read, 'Pro-

Mustang Mk IA armed with cannon for ground support and interdiction roles. Substitution of the Merlin for the Allison power plant allowed the P-51 to come to the front of the stage

Above: 'Zero altitude' attacks prove outstandingly successful. Below: Pilots train for the dangerous extreme low-level flying technique in California

ceed inland to road "Z". Patrol road "Z" from point 42 to point 38. Report any enemy action. Do not engage enemy aircraft unless necessary. Attack if enemy advance indicated. Maintain altitude zero.'

The pilots checked their charts, picked up a thin brown ribbon of road then dived to within ten feet of it. A swirl of dust rose to meet them as they levelled off and roared along its winding route. Suddenly a column of troops appeared before them. The Germans sighted the Mustangs at the same instant and threw themselves into the ditches on either side of the road in great confusion.

The pilots hauled back on the stick to avoid them, then put the Mustangs into a steep dive and nosed down towards the deck once more with throttles wide open. The Germans were just picking themselves up off the ground and brushing their uniforms when the Mustangs came again with guns blazing. Men began to scream and fall like tenpins as spurts of dust

Fw 190, a worthy opponent for the Mustang

jumped from the road. One death dealing swath and the Mustangs were gone.

As the planes climbed and began to circle over point 38 a warning crackled over the radio. 'Tallyho! Looks like a Focke Wulf coming in from the north. Get going.'

The Mustangs headed for the deck and then another Focke Wulf was sighted coming in from behind them. The snub nosed 190s started a long, gradual dive but the Mustangs hugged the ground and pushed the throttles wide open. The German pilot decided not to press the attack and broke off.

Their mission done, the two Mustangs pulled up in a tight bank. The pursuing Focke Wulf was then sighted ahead and one Mustang dove back for the deck while the other climbed to come up on his tail. As the range narrowed to 150 yards, the Mustang pilot opened fire and raked the 190

Camera installation in RAF P-51s makes possible vital photo-reconnaissance work over Europe

from stem to stern. Then at the moment of victory a Spitfire dived in from above and finished the 190 off with cannon fire. A gush of smoke and flame burst from the Focke Wulf and it crashed into the ground. The Mustangs joined up and headed for home.

One Mustang on the mission ran into heavy flak and had three feet of its port wing ripped off. The pilot applied full throttle and sped home. He landed some forty miles an hour faster than his normal landing speed. The runway was not long enough so he slowed as best he could before applying full brakes which set the craft up on its nose bending the propeller. The pilot was not hurt and the Mustang was soon repaired.

During this period Mustangs did fine work in the photographic-reconnaissance field. Using the camera

mounted behind the pilot, the aircraft would sweep in over the Dutch or French coast and get excellent low level photos of enemy installations. This constant surveillance proved to be invaluable in not only commando raids, such as Dieppe, but notably the tremendous task of keeping the Allied commanders aware of the coastal defenses during the planning of the invasion of the Continent in June of 1944.

In late 1942 the Mustang Is entered a new phase of activity against the Germans – locomotive busting. The pilots were not allowed to shoot up passenger trains for fear of injuring civilians in the occupied countries, but freight trains were legal targets.

On 13th October, 1942, F/O H H Hills and P/O F J Champlin of the RCAF crossed the French coast north of Le Havre where they caught a large engine pulling forty freight and twenty

Rail depots and freight trains are prime targets

tank cars. As they opened up on the engine, steam began to pour out and there was an explosion in the cab. Later in the month, Hills damaged another train but his Mustang was hit by light flak and he had to limp home with a tail assembly that was literally shredded.

From the moment of its initiation to combat the Mustang had amazed the British with the amount of punishment that it could take and still come home. As one pilot who flew the aircraft during the early days expressed it, 'These crates are amazing. They always seem to bring us back. It's the best ship in the world for the job we've got to do.'

Optimism as to the range of the Mustang I was proven in October 1942 when an RAF squadron flew between 600 and 700 miles to hit targets on the Dortmund-Ems canal in Germany. The attack was initiated over Holland where they shot up a military camp. Proceeding on into Germany, the Mustangs swept down on a factory at the gas depot at Lathen. Continuing on across the canal they scored hits on barges and a 500-ton ship was left burning in the Zuyder Zee.

Perhaps this long range strike was prompted by the ingenuity of Flight-Lieutenant J Lewkowicz, a Polish pilot who was flying Mustangs with No 309 Squadron. This pilot was a graduate engineer who in his spare time had carefully figured the minimum fuel consumption of the aircraft in relation to revolutions per minute and boost pressure on the engine to obtain maximum range. His calculations showed that the Mustang was capable of flying from his base in Scotland to Norway and back.

Repeatedly he put in request to HQ to prove his point, but no reply was forthcoming. On 27th September, 1942,

A Canadian Air Force Mustang. US Army Air Force was impressed enough with the aircraft's potential to earmark a sizeable fraction of initial production for its own use

25

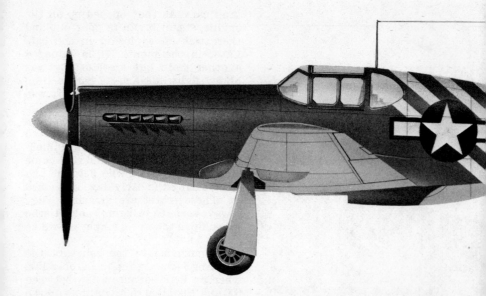

The North American P-51A Mustang was the last production model with an Allison engine. This had been used originally as it was available in large quantities in the United States and seemed to suit the Mustang to US requirements, but it had been found, as soon as the Mustang entered service, that the low-altitude rated Allison hampered the Mustang as an all purpose fighter. Consequently, it was used as a tactical reconnaissance and ground attack fighter, roles in which the Mustang's great speed and manoeuvrability at low altitude served it admirably. *Engine:* Allison V-1710-81 inline, 1,200hp at take off. *Armament:* Four Browning MG 53-2 machine guns with 350 rounds (inner pair) and 280 rounds (outer pair), plus two 250-, 325- or 500-lb bombs. *Speed:* 390mph at 20,000 feet. *Climb:* 9.1 minutes to 20,000 feet. *Ceiling:* 31,350 feet. *Range:* 750 miles clean and 2,350 miles with two 125-gallon drop tanks. *Weight empty/loaded:* 6,433/10,600lb *Span:* 37 feet 0¼ inches. *Length:* 32 feet 2½ inches. *Role:* Medium altitude fighter-bomber. Apart from its engine, the P-51A's main drawback was pilot visibility, which was poor as a result of the high rear fuselage decking and the heavy metal framing for the cockpit canopy. Deliveries of the P-51A began in March 1943

he set off on his own initiative to prove his theory. Lewkowicz took off from Scotland, flew to Norway, attacked enemy installations in the Stavanger region and returned safely. For his remarkable feat he was both reprimanded and congratulated. His findings made possible more distant sorties for the Mustang.

In November 1942, 309 Polish Squadron was transferred south to Gatwick where it was assigned reconnaissance duties over enemy fortifications in the Harvre-Boulogne sector. From their new base the Mustangs

set out in pairs to carry out their missions. The Channel crossing was made right on the deck. Once the coast was reached the leader of the pair would pull up to 900 feet and take his photographs with a long focus camera. His wingman would fly above keeping a lookout for enemy fighters. The actual taking of the photograph never lasted over three minutes and was performed at full throttle. Once the pictures were taken the Mustangs would drop down to minimum altitude and streak for home base.

The US Army Air Force had begun

British application 'Mustang'.

The whole world had been greatly impressed with the success of the vaunted German dive bomber, the Junkers Ju 87 'Stuka'. While time would prove that the Stuka was no match for any good fighter plane in the air, it had made its mark and the news bulletins of the early years of the war had made their impression on military minds as well. The US Army Air Force was no exception.

In spring 1942 funds had been appropriated for a dive bomber to be used in the invasion of North Africa. The dive bomber designs that had been approved by the War Department for use by the AAF did not perform to expectations and engineers at North American set out to see what could be done about modifying the Mustang into a fighter-bomber.

Hydraulically actuated dive flaps were fitted onto the trailing edge of the wing, bomb racks were fastened on the underside of the wings and the Allison V-1710-87 engine which provided high performance below 12,000 feet was installed in the aircraft. This modification proved successful in its tests and a contract was let for 500 planes in this version which was designated the A-36.

While other fighters had been adap-

to recognise the potentialities of the Mustang while it was being outfitted for the RAF as the Mustang Mark I and IA, and it held up delivery on fifty-seven of the initial aid contract for 150 aircraft. As a result of the outstanding performance of the Mustang as a reconnaissance aircraft in Europe the Army Air Force had the majority of their contingent modified for photo work. These aircraft were originally designated P-51-1NA and the name 'Apache' was assigned. However, the designation of the modified aircraft became F-6A and the name 'Apache' soon gave way to the

Stukas of the Luftwaffe; modified as the A-36, the Mustang filled a similar dive-bombing role for the Allies

A-36s take over a North African field.
Wreckage of the previous tenants
testifies to the Mustang's qualities

ted to bomb from a glide, they could
not dive vertically. The A-36 with its
dive brakes could come straight down
at an angle of ninety degrees to the
surface. Where the conventional dive
brake had a flap with circular slots,
the A-36s looked much like a picnic
grill. From the clash of the grill surface and the air stream the plane got
one of its most valuable weapons – its
scream. It rose from a low moan, as
the dive brakes were opened, to an ear
splitting wail when the bombs were
released. As the A-36 hurtled towards
its victim, a blood-curdling scream
would deafen him.

The A-36 arrived in North Africa too
late for the Tunisian campaign. When
it was received and put into service by
the 27th and 86th Fighter Bomber
Groups, the aerial assault of the
island of Pantelleria was underway.
These operations began in June 1943

and the dive bombing efforts of the
aircraft proved to be an immediate
success.

Normally the A-36s would orbit their
bombing target at an altitude of
approximately 12,000 feet. They
would then get in trail formation and
dive down one after the other on the
target. Bomb release was at approximately 3,000 feet at a speed of 290-300
miles per hour using full dive flaps.
Pull out was usually accomplished
by 1,500 feet. The aircraft proved to be
a very accurate bomber with the
capability of knocking out any type
of ground target.

With its two .50 caliber machine
guns mounted in the nose and two .50s
in each wing, the A-36 also presented a
formidable strafing weapon for use
once its dive bombing mission was
over. The A-36 would fly right down
on the deck and with the whining
pitch of the in-line engine it would be
right on top of enemy troop columns
or installations before he knew it.

As a result of the heavy bombing

and strafing attacks the island of Pantelleria capitulated in late June of 1943. The A-36s immediately moved onto the air bases there to operate against targets in Sicily in preparation for the invasion of this major enemy island bastion in the Mediterranean.

On 10th July, 1943, Allied troops stormed ashore in Sicily. Overhead were all the aircraft available for their support and the A-36s were right there with them. With their machine guns synchronised to mass their fire at 200-225 yards they proved most effective against the enemy.

On a typical day Captain Roger Miller was flying a ground support mission when several columns of troop trucks were sighted. 'They were carrying twenty to twenty-five men apiece,' stated Miller, 'they were probably German and put up a lot of flak which was very accurate. I didn't think we'd get through, but we did.

After that we saw a train carrying tanks on flat cars. It was in a railroad gorge near Aeia. We made three passes to get in to strafe them, then had a hell of a time getting out. It was one long pull and no picnic. Then we came back to strafe a column of trucks.

'A little farther up we ran into another locomotive pulling flat cars loaded with tanks. We shot up the tanks and blew up the locomotive. It was really a sight to see. The locomotive just went up in steam. About two miles farther we found another locomotive with six tanks and guns all around it. I saw the engineer get out in a hurry. We got that one, too.'

On a later mission that day Lieutenant J B Walton and his flight went after a convoy of some seventy-five trucks. The lead truck went off into a ditch to avoid the A-36s and Walton

Defensive precautions on the Sicilian beachhead

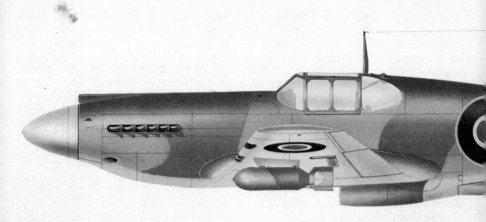

The North American A-36A Invader was a dive-bomber development of the P-51 Mustang. It was fitted with dive brakes under the wings, but these were wired up in the closed position in action. Deliveries started in September 1942 and finished in March 1943 after 500 had been delivered. The type first saw action in Sicily and Italy in 1943. The type flew 23,373 missions, dropped 8,014 tons of bombs, destroyed 17 enemy aircraft on the ground and 84 in the air for a loss of 177 of its own number. *Engine:* Allison V-1710-87 inline, 1,325hp at 3,000 feet. *Armament:* Six Browning MG 53-2 .5-inch machine guns and two 500-lb bombs. *Speed:* 356mph clean and 310mph with two bombs at 5,000 feet. *Ceiling:* 25,100 feet. *Range:* 550 miles. *Weight empty/loaded:* 6,100/ 10,700lbs. *Span:* 37 feet 0¼ inch. *Length:* 32 feet 2½ inches. One A-36A was supplied to Britain for experimental purposes

Below: A-36 'Invader', called, because of its quiet Allison engine, 'The Whispering Death' by the Germans

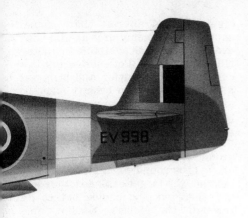

and swept the crew off with a short burst. Then he pulled up and sped from the area.

From the time of their initial combat the A-36s had been publicised as P-51s. This was unacceptable to the fighter-bomber pilots who were reluctant to be filed as P-51 or Mustang pilots. A new name that was more appropriate to their job was sought for by the pilots. After several suggestions, Lieutenant Robert Walsh spoke up, 'What's the matter with calling it the Invader? They're using us right now to invade Sicily. Some day not too long from now we'll be invading Europe.'

The other pilots around agreed and the name stuck. A short time later official sanction was granted and the A-36 became the Invader.

The A-36s did not often run into enemy fighters over Sicily, but Captain Tom Thomas was one of the few that did. The A-36 pilot was leading a group of planes over central Sicily when a lone German fighter came in. Thomas quickly got into position on

sprayed him with lead. As he swung over to the side of a mountain he was skirting he sighted two trucks carrying about thirty men each. The troops began to bail off the trucks just as Walton opened up on them. A locomotive was then sighted and Walton lined up on it and hit the gun button. A full burst into the boiler left it standing with steam spewing from a bevy of holes. Some flak started to blossom in the area at this time as the gunners fired at the American fighter-bombers in the area. Walton came in on the gun emplacement from the blind side

This A-36 over Vesuvius shows the profile similarity to the Bf 109

his tail and shot him from the sky. But suddenly he was aware of smoking tracers and he began to take hits in his aircraft. Desperately he pulled up to get some altitude and he went over the side at only 300 feet. The parachute just had time to open before his canopy caught on a building as he landed in the back end of a truck. He was immediately surrounded by Italians and there was nothing he could do but surrender. With burns on his face and legs and a broken leg he was taken to the hospital. The Italians failed to transport him out to Italy and he was liberated when the Americans took Palermo.

As Allied forces proceeded to smash forward and overrun Sicily the A-36 groups moved to advanced bases on the island. From these bases the Invaders were able to fly many more missions and to give added cover to the ground forces. Strangely enough, they were also aided greatly by the Sicilians who had no love for the Germans. On numerous occasions, the civilians on the ground would point out to the low flying fighters the positions of camouflaged enemy positions. The fighter-bombers would take over from there.

The pilots learned to make the most of the element of surprise when attacking ground installations. More than one pilot learned the hard way that the Germans were very accurate on machine gun and pom-pom batteries. The golden rule seemed to be: once the first pass had been made, never, never, go back for a second pass unless all but entire destruction had been effected the first time.

By the end of August 1943, the campaign in Sicily was all but over. Attacks were initiated against the Italian mainland in preparation for the invasion. On the morning of 3rd September, Allied troops hit the beaches of Italy. Both groups of A-36s were in the air covering the beachhead, bombing gun installations and attacking ground targets.

There is no more difficult task for a single-engined aircraft than ground support. The enemy fires at him with everything he has available including rifles and pistols. For such aircraft to survive this opposition and bring its pilot safely back to base it must be able to take a maximum amount of punishment. The A-36 was exceptional in its ability to fulfill this rôle.

One A-36 pilot was coming in over a ground target in Italy only forty feet above the ground when he hit his gun button. The target exploded violently and there was no choice but to fly through the debris. Shells came through the floor of the cockpit, but luckily none hit the pilot. The wings were peppered and the ailerons were all but blown off. Large holes up to six inches in diameter were blown in the wings and the metal skin was peeled up and jagged.

There were holes in every square foot of the wings and the right wing tip was partly torn loose and pointed upwards. The horizontal stabilisers were bent upwards and full of holes and the leading edge of the left horizontal stabiliser was completely blown away. The rudder and elevators were still controlable, but aileron control was described as 'sloppy'. The cockpit was filled with smoke and the instruments were hardly visible but the pilot noticed that the altimeter read 1,200 feet.

After flying approximately twenty miles, the engine cut out, so the pilot bailed out. Once in the water he began to swim for shore but he was quickly picked up by an Italian speed boat. He was taken to a small island offshore and turned over to American paratroops who had taken the island a few days before.

Not all pilots were so lucky. One flight of four Invaders went into strafe a line of forty enemy box cars sitting on a rail siding. As one pilot gave them a burst from his six .50 caliber machine guns a tremendous explosion took place. Apparently the cars had been loaded with ammunition. This A-36 disintegrated in mid-air. So

Above: Allied landings on the Italian mainland are followed by the massive supplies build-up. *Below:* A mild example of the kind of condition in which the tough P-51 often limped home

violent was the blast that his comrades' aircraft were riddled and twisted. All three were fortunate enough to limp home.

Even over Italy the Invaders seldom tangled with enemy fighters. The primary reason for this was the fact that the A-36s were engaged in dive bombing and ground support and unless the enemy sought to intercept them they rarely saw any German fighters. However, the Luftwaffe had suffered enough at the hands of the A-36s to realise they were formidable opponents at low altitude. The Invaders could out-run and out-maneuver the German fighters and often they did. Over the Salerno beachhead the A-36s accounted for over a dozen German fighters for the loss of only one of their own in aerial combat.

Shortly after the invasion, four Invader pilots were called upon to fly a most unusual mission. A number of American paratroops were cut off and without supplies. It was the job of Lieutenant J B Walton and three other pilots of the 524th Fighter-Bomber Squadron to fly food and ammunition in to them. The packages were heavily wrapped and slung on the bomb racks. So heavily loaded were the aircraft that they barely got airborne.

Once the location of the Americans had been ascertained the A-36s swooped down and released their loads with pin-point accuracy. The desperately-needed supplies enabled the paratroops to hold out until a relief party could fight its way through to them. Yet another mission had been found for the versatile Invader.

On 10th September, 1943, the 27th Fighter-Bomber Group's ground support activities reached its zenith. American troops were coming ashore at Salerno when the call for help came. Three German panzer divisions were rushing to the scene in a desperate attempt to throw the invasion forces into the sea. The A-36s were loaded with bombs and ammunition to intercept the onrushing German armored column. From early morning until that night the A-36s roared up and down the road bombing and machine-gunning the enemy. So outstanding was the work of the 27th Group that day that they were awarded a Distinguished Unit Citation.

The job of ground support continued for the Invader pilots throughout the subsequent invasion at Anzio on the road to Rome. The A-36 continued to do yeoman duty until the weary aircraft were replaced in early spring 1944. Reluctantly, the pilots went to work flying the much larger and heavier P-47. Those who put their time in on the A-36 would never forget their faithful mounts that had carried them into battle and home again so many times, nor would the Germans ever forget the 'screaming demon' that rained his bombs upon them.

When Eighth Air Force was intially formed in Britain there had been no real serious consideration given to the problem of fighter escort for the heavy bombers. As a matter of fact in 1942 General Arnold, Commanding General of the US Army Air Force, sent a cablegram to Major-General James E Cheney stating that five groups of pursuit (later to be called fighter) groups would be dispatched to Britain. Two were to be utilised in defense of Northern Ireland and three would form the striking force against the German air force.

However, when the plans were drawn up for the actual operations of the B-17s flying from Britain it was decided that tactics would be worked out with the American fighters whereby they would furnish escort to the bombers to the extent of their endurance. From there the defense of the bomber formations would be dependant on the close defensive formation flying of the individual units.

In spring 1942, Cheney learned that the only types of fighters available for the initial missions of the soon-to-arrive B-17s would be Curtiss P-40s and Bell P-39s. He seriously doubted the ability of these types of aircraft to

perform escort duty and put the question to Air-Marshal Portal of the RAF. It was his suggestion to equip the American fighter units with Spitfires. He also advised the shipping of a like number of P-40s to the Middle East for operations with the British. He considered the Spitfire the 'best all-round fighter developed in this war, which readily adapts itself to the mission of providing top cover for bombardment missions within its range.'

Portal's advise was taken and when the first American fighter group, the 31st, arrived in June 1942 it was equipped with Spitfires and commenced combat training. Shortly afterwards elements of the 1st Fighter Group began to arrive in P-38s and while they were permitted to keep their aircraft, they also entered intensive combat training under the tutelage of the RAF.

On 17th August, 1942, twelve B-17s from the 97th Bomb Group flew the

Above: P-47 Thunderbolts replaced A-36s in Italy in spring 1944. *Below:* Air Marshal Sir Charles Portal

General Carl Spaatz (left) with
General Arnold

first heavy bomb mission from their base in England. Under heavy fighter cover furnished by RAF Spitfires, the Flying Fortresses struck at marshalling yards at Rouen and Sotteville in France. Three Messerschmitt 109s were sighted watching the formation but they made no attempt to attack the bombers.

The success of the mission caused for optimism in American circles. General Carl Spaatz reported to Arnold that he felt that the enemy did not press his attacks on the bombers due to the concentration of firepower potential of the close formation maintained and the presence of escorting fighters. However, the moot question was still unanswered. Could the heavy bombers venture deep into enemy territory beyond the range of the escorting fighters and escape without heavy losses?

In late August the 52nd Fighter Group arrived and this unit was assigned to fly Spitfires. Shortly afterwards they were joined by the P-38s of the 14th Fighter Group. At this time the VIII Fighter Command could claim four groups in various stages of combat-readiness.

The former Eagle Squadrons of the RAF, composed of American volunteer pilots transferred to the VIII Fighter Command on 29th September, 1942, giving the US Air Force another three Spitfire squadrons with which to operate. However, the coming invasion of North Africa drastically changed the plans of the Eighth Air Force. The 1st and 14th Fighter Group's P-38s and the Spitfires of the 31st and 52nd Group were reassigned to the new Twelfth Air Force which would move to North Africa.

The P-38s did get in a few escort missions before their departure, but it fell the task of the 4th Fighter Group's former Eagle Squadrons and Spitfires of the RAF to furnish escort to the bombers during the latter part of 1942. However, the departure of the P-38s was a serious blow to the bombers for the Spitfire could take them only to the fighter belt of the Luftwaffe on the French coast while the Lightnings could take them much further inland.

With the departure of the P-38s and the onset of winter the missions of the Eighth Air Force bombers decreased markedly. Only eight missions were flown in November 1942 and this was cut in half during December. All of these missions were flown against targets on the French coast. Some of these targets such as Saint Nazaire housed the German U-boat pens and to strike them the bombers had to fly out from under the protective umbrella of Spitfires and a number of Fortresses began to fall to the guns of Luftwaffe fighters.

Regardless, the VIII Bomber Command still contended in a report written late in 1942 that: 'One salient fact emerges from any study of German fighter tactics against missions flown to date. No tactics have been evolved capable of inflicting uneconomical losses on units of twelve or more B-17s or B-24s when flown in close formation.'

Of course, VIII Bomber Command had no way of determining the reasons behind the limited opposition that the Luftwaffe had put up against the American bomber formations to that point. First, the Germans were probing the bomber formations to determine their defensive capabilities. Secondly, the shallow penetration missions were very heavily escorted and the Luftwaffe did not chose to come in contact with the Allied fighters. Thirdly, the Germans did not feel that the raids against the Channel

The long-range Lightning is badly missed when withdrawn from escort duties; German pilots avoided the distinctive P-38

The P-47 Thunderbolt proved a match for the Fw 190 at altitude but assumed a more defensive role in low-level action

coast targets were affecting their war effort to any great extent. Fourthly, the German mass production of fighters had not reached the point where new aircraft were coming off the lines in great quantity and the vast majority of their operational units were tied up on other fronts. Lastly, the Luftwaffe was just beginning to organise their defenses in the west. As late as 1942 the Germans had only about 100 fighters based along the western coast from the Heligoland Bight to Biarritz.

On Christmas Eve 1942 the VIII Fighter Command received the first of a fighter design that would carry out the brunt of escort operations during 1943. The heavy, blunt nosed, radial engined Republic P-47 had come to England. Air Force interest and speculation as to its performance had been the primary cause of the lack of interest in the early Mustang design at Wright Field testing base and great faith had been placed in this fighter.

The P-47-C had an internal fuel capacity of 305 gallons, 205 in the main tank and another 100 gallons in an internal auxiliary tank, giving it a maximum escort range of about 175 miles. With external tanks the aircraft was capable of giving protection to the bombers some 200 miles beyond the enemy coast, but the aircraft arrived in England without external fuel tanks.

Performance-wise, the P-47 was pitted against a Focke Wulf 190, German-built fighter, shortly after its arrival. The massive Thunderbolt was able to hold its own dogfighting the Focke Wulf above 15,000 feet, but at low altitude it was unable to stay with the lighter more agile craft. The P-47 also lacked climbing performance. It could not climb as swiftly as either the Focke Wulf or the Messerschmitt 109. But with its massive radial engine

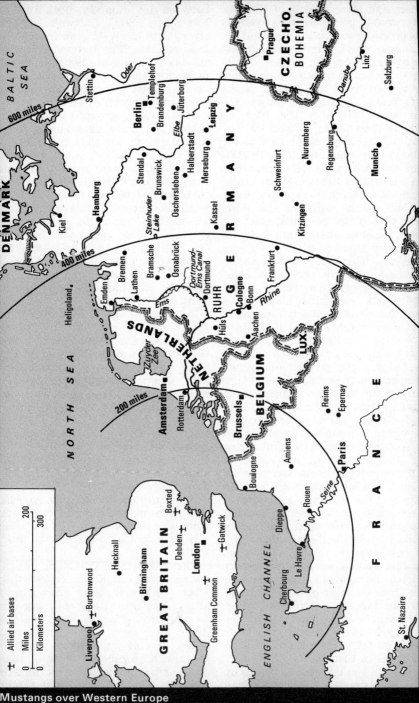

Mustangs over Western Europe

in the nose, it could dive with the best of them and later models of the aircraft would incorporate a paddle blade propeller and water injection for the engine which improved performance considerably.

However, its high altitude performance initially made the P-47 an excellent aircraft for bomber escort. Its main limitation was the lack of available drop tanks to feed the big Pratt and Whitney engine that had a tendancy to gobble fuel. Initially 200-gallon drop tanks were imported from the United States. These tanks were made of resinated paper and were attached to the belly of the P-47. These proved to be unsatisfactory chiefly because fuel could not be drawn from them at altitudes above 23,000 feet. They also proved to be leaky and caused a very high aerodynamic drag on the aircraft.

The P-47s struggled along with these tanks until 108-gallon paper tanks were manufactured in Britain and became available in July 1943. These tanks had a pressurisation feature, but quantity production did not commence until September of 1943.

During the summer months three fighter groups, the 4th, 56th and 78th, flew P-47s and carried the brunt of escort duty. They did an excellent job of overcoming their initial difficulties with the Thunderbolt and carrying the air war into enemy territory to the limit of their endurance. Yet the planners of the combined air offensive desired that the strategic bombing program be carried deep into enemy territory where the P-47s could not go. The best they could do with what they had was to send fighter escort out with the bombers only to have to leave them on their own to continue on to the target. A second escorting force would be dispatched later in the day to pick up the bombers on their return and bring them safely back to their bases in Britain.

In view of the increased attacks by Allied bombers the Luftwaffe began its build-up in the west. Fighter pro-duction was given first priority and between 1st January, 1943 and 1st November, 1943, Luftwaffe fighter strength in the West grew from 670 to 1,660 aircraft. The Luftwaffe created six day-fighter areas between Trondheim and Hendaye and developed a very efficient radar system to warn of approaching Allied aircraft.

Pilots were regrouped to bring the better and more experienced flyers into Germany for the air defense of the greater Reich. Many of their veteran pilots were also pulled into the homeland from the Russian front to bolster defenses. Once the P-47s began to venture into Germany major air battles began to develop and bomber losses began to increase. On 17th April, 1943, 106 American bombers attacked Bremen of which sixteen were lost on one of the first missions on which the Thunderbolts went into Germany.

In June 1943 the VIII Bomber Command ventured into Germany without fighter escort and suffered high losses. Of sixty B-17s attacking Kiel on 13th June, twenty-two were downed primarily due to heavy fighter attacks. Messerschmitt 109s, Focke Wulf 190s, Messerschmitt 110s and even Junkers Ju 88s attacked the formation with bitter intensity. The fighters came screaming in on head-on passes while the twin-engined Messerschmitt 110s and Junkers Ju 88s sat out of machine gun range and fired their 20mm cannon into the formations. Another sixteen bombers fell eight days later when the rubber plant of I G Farben was attacked at Huls in the Ruhr Valley.

The VIII Bomber Command went to Oschersleben and Kassel on 28th July where they met fierce enemy opposition. The operations that day cost twenty-two B-17s and losses would no doubt have been higher had not 105 P-47s carrying jettisonable tanks for the first time gone out to meet them on their way home 250 miles from the coast of England. The fighters surprised one group of about sixty Ger-

Luftwaffe Fighter Organisation

Jagdgeschwader (Usual operational unit of about 120 aircraft: divided into three 'Gruppen')

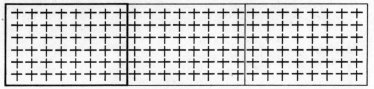

Gruppe – the normal fighting unit (divided into 12-aircraft 'Staffeln')

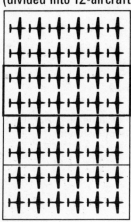

Staffel (divided into three 4-aircraft 'Schwärme')

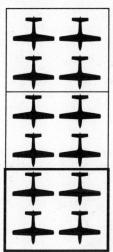

Rotte

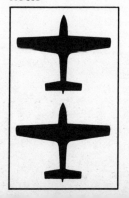

Schwarm (split into 2-aircraft 'Rotten')

Above: B-17s were severely mauled in the Kiel raid of June 1943. *Below:* Some were lucky and returned despite taking considerable punishment

man fighters picking on bomber cripples and managed to shoot down nine of them before combat was broken off.

In its most ambitious effort of summer 1943 the VIII Bomber Command launched a double mission deep into Germany on 16th August. Initially 146 B 17s were airborne on a bombing mission directed at the Messerschmitt assembly plant at Regensburg. Eighteen squadrons of P-47s and sixteen squadrons of RAF Spitfires were assigned to escort the bombers as far as their range permitted. Once the escort had to leave them the bombers went on to the target alone and proceeded to fly on to American bases in North Africa. Although their bombing results were quite good the Flying Fortresses were under almost constant attack from the time the fighters left them until they surprisingly continued on towards the Mediterranean. Of 127 bombers attacking twenty-four were lost.

Three and a half hours after the departure of the Regensburg force another force of 230 Fortresses set out to bomb the ball-bearing works at Schweinfurt. The mission had been staggered in order that the fighters might return from one escort mission and be refueled to escort the second force.

However, this also gave the Luftwaffe fighters time to land, refuel, rearm and get back into the air. Thirty-six of the B-17s on the Schweinfurt strike were lost to bring a monstrous total of sixty American bombers lost for the day. This comprised 19% of the attacking force for both missions. Had the one bomb division not continued on to Africa, no doubt the losses would have been higher for they would have had to fight their way back to a point where the escort could pick them up.

Long range escort was able to demonstrate its capabilities on 27th September, 1943, when the P-47s were able to take the bombers all the way to Emden. With the aid of 75-gallon drop tanks the Thunderbolts made the entire trip into Germany. Bomber losses dropped to only seven of the 244 that attacked the target. The P-47s claimed twenty-one enemy fighters for a loss of only two of their own.

As long as the fighters were able to go with the B-17s or B-24s, losses were relatively light, but whenever the bombers ventured deep into enemy territory they rose astronomically. The climax came in October 1943 when the B-17s returned to the ball-bearing plants at Schweinfurt. On the 14th, 291 B-17s were dispatched from the two Fortress divisions. The two forces crossed the enemy coast abreast, some thirty miles apart. P-47s gave escort as far as their fuel permitted and then the B-17s were on their own. When this force departed in the vicinity of Aachen, some 240 miles from the British coast, the Luftwaffe attacked in swarms.

Every type of aircraft that was capable of interception took part.

In the skies over an 8th Air Force fighter base in England, Mustangs peel off to land

The bombers absorbed terrific punishment from head-on and overhead passes. Twin-engine aircraft came at the Fortresses tail-on and lobbed shells into the formation. Even air to air bombing was attempted.

Sixty of the VIII Bomber Command B-17s fell to anti-aircraft fire and fighter attacks that day. Another seventeen Fortresses sustained major damage and another 121 were damaged.

German Quartermaster records confirm the loss of only thirty-eight Luftwaffe fighters and twenty damaged during the air battle. Fortunately VIII Fighter Command Thunderbolts and RAF Spitfires went out to meet the bedraggled force on its way back and escorted them on to England. Despite optimistic claims regarding damage done to the target, it suffered only a temporary setback.

The Eighth Air Force was now faced with a drastic decision. With such tremendous losses could the daylight bombing campaign continue? Without

escorting fighters the losses had become prohibitive. A few P-38s were becoming available in the theater and their two 75-gallon drop tanks enabled them to have a maximum escort radius of 520 miles, but even with the 108-gallon drop tanks that were available in the early autumn of 1943 the Thunderbolts could do no better than a 375-miles radius at the very most. The rugged P-47 had done a tremendous job of beating the Luftwaffe in the skies where it was permitted to go, but its range was just not sufficient at the time.

In November 1943 the first P-51 Mustang fighter unit arrived on the scene. However, much to the chagrin of VIII Fighter Command the new charges were assigned to the newly transferred Ninth Air Force. Major General William Kepner of VIII Fighter Command got around this by means of an agreement whereby the support and protection of the heavy bombers became the primary role of all US fighter units based in Britain. For all practical purposes the P-51s of the 9th Air Force belonged to VIII Fighter Command for some months.

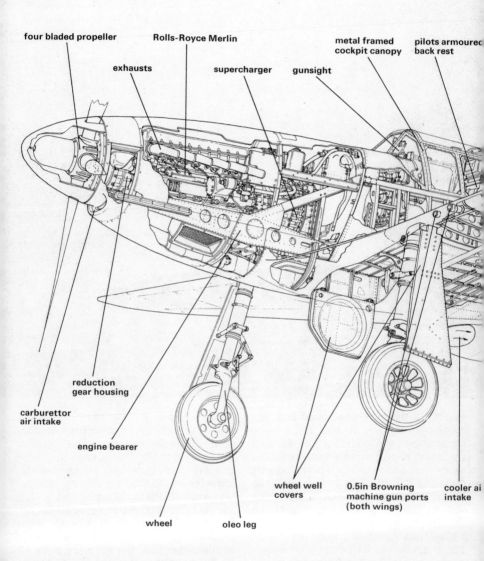

four bladed propeller

Rolls-Royce Merlin

metal framed
cockpit canopy

pilots armoured
back rest

exhausts

supercharger

gunsight

reduction
gear housing

carburettor
air intake

engine bearer

wheel well
covers

0.5in Browning
machine gun ports
(both wings)

cooler ai
intake

wheel

oleo leg

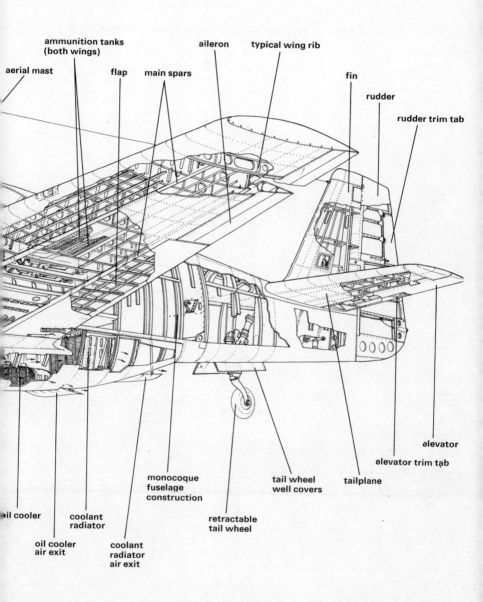

ammunition tanks
(both wings)

aileron

typical wing rib

aerial mast

flap

main spars

fin

rudder

rudder trim tab

oil cooler

coolant
radiator

oil cooler
air exit

coolant
radiator
air exit

monocoque
fuselage
construction

retractable
tail wheel

tail wheel
well covers

tailplane

elevator trim tab

elevator

The long reach

The aircraft that was to arrive in Britain as the original long range escort fighter evolved through the marriage of the North American Mustang airframe to the Packard Motor Corporation built Rolls Royce Merlin engine. Packard had negotiated to begin manufacture of the engine during the summer of 1940 when Great Britain was eagerly seeking American assistance in the acquisition of aircraft and engines. Production lines were set up in an unused building in Detroit for the American manufacture of the Merlin XX engine. The initial model of this 12-cylinder 'V' type in-line engine was designated the V-1650 engine by the US Army Air Force. First engines began coming off the line in September 1941 and these were utilised in the Curtiss P-40-F aircraft.

Testing of the Mustang Mark I by Fighter Command of the RAF had brought forth the comment that the maneuverability and range of the aircraft were excellent but what it really needed for high altitude performance was the Merlin engine. Major Tommy Hitchcock, an American Air Attaché in London at the time, began to push for modification to be made to the aircraft for American production with the British engine.

In spring 1942 four Mustangs were turned over to the Rolls Royce facility at Hucknall where modifications were made to mate the Merlin engine to the aircraft. Coolant requirements of the Merlin engine necessitated a larger radiator installation. Ducting was changed with a Spitfire beard type intake installed below the engine. A four-bladed Rotol propeller was installed to compensate for the increased power of the 1,520hp Merlin.

British testing began in October of 1942 and proved most impressive. The Mustang's final performance figures

The XP-51B, a P-51A modified to take the Packard-built Rolls Royce engine. Eventually no further Allison-engined Mustangs were produced

Above: Brand new Mustangs await shipment at the Los Angeles factory. *Below:* Assembly lines at the Dallas factory. Mustangs originating here bear the designation P-51C-NT

showed a top speed of 432 miles per hour at 22,000 feet, utilizing the supercharger in high blower position. The British test pilot was most enthusiastic about the landing qualities of the aircraft. The only edge that the British Spitfire held over the newly modified Mustang was the ability to turn inside of it. Results of the testing were immediately sent to both the US Army Air Force and to North American Aviation.

Meanwhile, the Packard-built Merlin engine had been mated to the Mustang by engineers at North American Aviation in California for testing. This had been brought about by a contract which had been placed by the US Army Air Force in August 1942 calling for 400 Merlin-powered Mustangs to be designated P-51B-1NA. Originally the Merlin-engined models were to have been designated P-78, but after the incorporation of Merlin engines in two Mustangs it was decided that no further Allison-powered aircraft would be built, so the XP-78 designation was dropped.

The first test flight of the American modified fighter took place on 30th November, 1942, with North American test pilot, Bob Chilton, at the controls. Excellent flight characteristics were reported, but the aircraft was forced to land after only forty-five minutes due to overheating of the engine. Radiator modifications were required and testing did not recommence until December of 1942. Final results showed a top speed of 441mph at 29,800 feet as compared to the Allison powered crafts 387mph at 15,000 feet. Improved performance in all departments was so significant that the aircraft was ordered into full mass production. The P-51B-NA was to be turned out at the North American facility at Inglewood, California, and a second plant was opened at Dallas, Texas. Dallas-built craft were to bear the designation P-51C-NT.

On 4th November 1943, a weary but exuberant t group of young American pilots checked into the airdrome at

Greenham Commons in Berkshire. These pilots comprised the 354th Fighter Group of the US Army Air Force. The vast majority of these men had no combat experience, but were fresh from the United States where they had trained on Bell P-39 Airacobras. As had been the custom with the new groups before them, they expected to be fitted out with Republic P-47s, but on arrival at Greenham Commons the word was officially given that they were to be the first American group in the European theater to be outfitted with the brand new P-51B Mustang.

The pilots of the 354th began to check out in P-51As of the 10th and 67th Reconnaissance Groups immediately and within a week that was virtually completed. On 11th November the first five P-51Bs arrived and once the pilots experienced its performance they were completely sold on the Mustang.

By mid-November the group moved to the base at Boxted near Colchester in Essex. Here they received the balance of their new Mustangs and began an intensive training program. The eyes of the 'top brass' of the Eighth Air Force were on this new Ninth Air Force fighter unit: with their long range potential of some 550 to 600 miles these aircraft could penetrate into Germany deeply enough to escort the bombers to any target on the list.

With only a few short weeks of operational training behind them, the 354th 'Pioneer Mustang' Group was scheduled for its first orientation over the coast of Belgium and down to Pas de Calais on 1st December. The mission was led by the veteran commander of the 4th Fighter Group, Colonel Don Blakeslee. Twenty-four Mustangs winged across the murky waters of the English Channel and flew along the coast where they observed for the first time the black, ugly puffs of smoke which eminated from the exploding anti-aircraft or flak shells. The mission took only an

hour and twenty minutes and was without incident or interception. However, the surfaces of some of the Mustangs had been holed by flak fragments; so it might be said the group was officially 'blooded' on its first mission.

The unit flew another short mission to the Amiens area of France on 5th December and on the 11th it flew its first bomber escort mission to Emden. Enemy aircraft were encountered, but no victims were claimed. However, the group suffered its first loss when one Mustang failed to return due to engine failure.

The 354th Group set out to escort the bombers to Kiel on 13th December and encountered a formation of Messerschmitt 110s. In this combat the first claim was made by Lieutenant Glenn T Eagleston in the following report:

Colonel Don Blakeslee, leader of the 364th 'Pioneer Mustang' Group's first mission

Lieutenant Glenn T Eagleston (to left of board) holds a briefing session in front of his aircraft. His was the first kill claimed by the 364th Group

'I was flying mutual support with Lt Emmer in two-ship formation en route to home base after participating in an escort mission over Kiel. I observed an Me 110 about 3,000 feet below and to starboard. I peeled off under Lt Emmer, with whom I had no radio communication. At this time we were at about 18,000 feet in the general vicinity of Frederick Stach.

'I made four passes at the e/a with the following results:

'No 1 fired short burst from ninety degrees closing to line astern 1,000 yards to 300 yards. Observed no strikes. Rear gunner fired just as I dragged into trail.

'No 2 fired 1½-second burst from 200 yards astern and from slightly above. Observed strikes on fuselage. Rear gunner discontinued fire during this engagement and never fired again.

'No 3 fired short burst from 300 yards astern and from slightly above. Knocked out right engine which burst into flame, parts flying off engine.

'No 4 came in from astern and slightly above but guns were jammed and broke off without firing.

'Enemy aircraft took no evasive action after second pass and when last observed was still in shallow glide, right engine dead and aflame heading through the overcast which was estimated at about 6,000 feet. I returned home alone.'

This claim went into the books and was officially logged as a 'probably destroyed' by Lieutenant Eagleston. This man was destined to become the top scoring ace of the Ninth Air Force with eighteen aerial victories to his credit.

The initial encounter of Lieutenant Eagleston brought to light a malfunction that would continue to plague Mustang pilots for some months. The four machine guns mounted in the wings of the P-51B were canted to such an angle that they were almost lying on their sides. When the aircraft became involved in maneuvers where high 'g' forces were applied the ammunition tended to congest in the feed chutes causing the guns to jam. Booster motors for the ammunition belts were installed as a stop-gap remedy but the problem was not really solved until later models of the Mustang incorporated the mounting of the guns in an upright position with booster motors installed.

Lieutenant Charles F Gumm scored the first official victory for the 354th Group and the AAF Mustang on an escort mission to Bremen on 16th December, 1943. Gumm and his wingman, Lieutenant Talbot, sighted four Messerschmitt 109s lining up behind a box of bombers and went up after them. The Luftwaffe pilots sighted

Gun camera pictures of the demise of a Bf 109. After this encounter pieces of the disintegrating aircraft were found lodged in the wings of the US fighter

the Mustangs and two of them broke down in an attempt by the Mustangs to go after them.

However, the American pilots were not to be deterred from their job and continued to climb after the two remaining Messerschmitts. As Talbot positioned himself to fire his prey broke left and down. Gumm continued to close rapidly on his victim while Talbot covered him. Gumm cut the gap to 100 yards before he opened fire. A two-second burst showed no visual effect, so Gumm pulled up to within fifty yards of the German aircraft. A three-second burst brought a thin trail of smoke from the engine. At very close range the young American pilot hit the gun button again and was rewarded with thick oil smoke and pieces flying back from the Messerschmitt. The German aircraft rolled off and down to the left, streaming smoke from its flaming engine. The Mustang pilot had drawn first blood.

After this first success, the Mustangs of the 354th began to score regularly. Their P-51s encountered large formations of Messerschmitt 109s and 110s on an escort mission to Kiel on 5th January, 1944, and sixteen of the enemy fell before their guns without the loss of a single one of their own.

Six days later another fifteen Luftwaffe fighters were downed in a massive air battle in the Halberstadt and Oschersleben area. The performance of the day was turned in by former Flying Tiger ace, Major James H Howard. When enemy fighters were first encountered the P-51s broke to attack and unceremoniously cut their leader, Major Howard, out of the attack pattern. The bombers were under fire from German fighters all over the sky and Howard sighted a lone box of bombers that were absorbing all the punishment that some forty enemy craft could apply.

Immediately Howard in his Mustang, 'Ding Hao', sped to the attack. First to get in his way was a Messer-

Ex-Flying Tiger pilot Jim Howard's P-51, spectacularly victorious in many encounters in early 1944

schmitt 110, twin-engined fighter, which took a few bursts from his guns, broke out in flames and crashed into the snow-covered terrain.

Howard then sighted a Focke Wulf 190 below him which pulled sunwards once he saw the P-51. Howard moved his plane up behind him, gave him a devestating burst from his four .50 caliber machine guns and watched the pilot bail out. A Messerschmitt 109 was the next to feel the wrath of Howard's guns. Its German pilot tried to get the P-51 to overrun him by dropping his flaps, but the Mustang pilot did likewise and stayed on the tail of the enemy aircraft. The 109 broke down trailing smoke from his engine.

Howard pulled back up with the bombers in time to sight another Me 110 upon which he immediately scored numerous hits. The German

fighter turned over on his back and nosed down towards the ground streaming black smoke. Another 109 was then sighted beginning to go into a pursuit curve attack on the bombers. Howard latched onto his tail and sent him diving for the deck with black smoke pouring from his engine.

On this attack three of Howard's machine guns had ceased to function. With only one gun he dove on another 109 and got strikes all over him. The German pilot splitessed and dived away out of the area.

The last enemy aircraft that Jim Howard encountered that day was a twin-engined Dornier Do 217 which was coming in alongside the bombers to discharge his rockets. The P-51 pilot dove on the Dornier and the German pilot decided not to attempt his attack even though Howard did not even fire at him.

The men aboard the bombers could not praise the unknown Mustang pilot enough. One of them expressed the encounter as, 'It was a case of one lone

American taking on the entire Luftwaffe.' When the pilot's identity was discovered and the public relations people descended on him all that the modest Howard would say was, 'I seen my duty and I done it.' The men aboard the bombers later confirmed six victories for Howard, but he would claim only two destroyed, two probables and two damaged. Nevertheless, Howard's superiors saw fit to award him the Congressional Medal of Honor for his feat.

As though weather, flak and enemy fighters were not troubles enough, the early Mustang pilots were plagued by identification problems. In silhouette the P-51 resembled the German Messerschmitt 109. Just as the pilots had experienced this trouble flying their Mustang Mark I over Britain the American pilots were having their troubles over the Continent. On a number of occasions the Mustangs of the 354th were jumped by P-47 Thun-

derbolt pilots. After a number of such encounters VIII Fighter Command put out a bulletin to its pilots advising close study of the recognition silhouettes of the two different aircraft in question.

One of those Mustang pilots who was shot up by a 'friendly' aircraft was Lieutenant Glen Eagleston:

'I was leading a three-ship flight on the Brunswick raid (February 10th, 1944). In the vicinity of Steinhuder Lake, I turned south to investigate a bogey (enemy aircraft). I then saw six Me 109s about 5,000 feet above us and into the sun and as I started a climbing turn for position for attack my flight was tapped by about eight P-47s. I saw a P-47 go by with an Me 109 on his tail and I went after the enemy air-

Despite their heavy defensive armament Fortresses were more than grateful for long-range Mustang support

craft, my wingman following me.

'As I maneuvered into position to fire I was attacked by a P-47 from astern, taking strikes through one wing and along the fuselage. I broke away and watched the P-47 for a minute and convinced that the P-47 had satisfied himself as to proper recognition dived to attack two Me 109s which were about 1,000 feet below and closing on the tail of my wingman.

'I closed rapidly on the one nearest and fired a long burst from 100 yards astern. I observed strikes on the fuselage. As I cleared my tail and circled, I saw my wingman firing at an M109 which seemed to explode and go out of control.

'My wingman rejoined me and I started for home as the engine was heating up. The oil pressure dropped to zero as I crossed the enemy coast and the engine froze as I crossed the English coast. I glided to 12,000 feet and went over the side at 11,500 feet, landing safely.'

However, this problem of identity worked two ways as Lieutenant Jack T Bradley, of the 354th Group found out one day.

'We were flying in a rather loose formation on a search party one day', he stated. 'I couldn't see the rest of my party, but I knew about where they were and it was no trouble for me to locate them with the radio. I called for one of my squadron to give me his location, which he readily did. Following his instructions, I came upon my squadron (I thought) and my place in the formation for a full three or four minutes.

'I casually took a glance out the side window and discovered I was flying in a formation of Messerschmitt 109s. They recognised me about the same time I found out who they were. I never saw so many black crosses in all of my life. I was surrounded.

'The Germans started after me, but I dropped my belly tanks and dived out of the formation. They soon saw that the Mustang was too fast for them so they returned to their formation'.

The 354th Group continued to score steadily on its escort missions as it went along with the bombers to targets such as Frankfurt and Brunswick. They had another big day on 11th February but the mission cost them their leader, Lieutenant-Colonel Kenneth R Martin. He went down after a mid-air collision.

'The Germans were attempting to keep us from getting to our rendezvous with the bombers,' stated Colonel Martin. 'First, they hit us from above when we passed the French Coast on the way in, then again when we were close to the bombers. Their radar could always put them on top of us. Usually they went for the bombers, but had realised they'd need to stop us before they get called to the bombers or they would be vulnerable from the rear while making their attack.

'On the second attack my wingman was shot down and I was able to get the 109 that got him. Finishing the quick circle after shooting down the 109, I saw another 109 approximately a mile away so I headed my plane toward him. He was in a slight turn and saw me coming toward him so he wheeled around and headed toward me. We both were firing in a head-on run. Due to our past gun trouble I looked at mine to see if they were firing as I did not seem to be hitting the target. However, they were firing as were the guns on the Messerschmitt. Guess my aim was poor and so was his. Anyway, the last I remembered was seeing the swastika on the side of the 109 on my right at the same level about ten feet out just as we hit.'

Miraculously, both Martin and the German pilot managed to clear their mangled aircraft and parachute safely to the ground. Martin was severely injured and remained a prisoner for the balance of the war in Europe.

However, his 'Pioneer Mustangs' did well that day. Fourteen victories were counted up for the group. On the same day Major Jim Howard led the second P-51 group to become operation-

Above: Fortresses approaching their target; fighter protection remains vital
Below: A fleeing Fw 190 receives a mortal wound over Germany

al from England. The 357th Fighter Group made their first sortie, which proved to be uneventful over the French coast.

20th February brought on the first mission of what was to become known in the Eighth Air Force as 'Big Week'. These missions' objective was to destroy the German aircraft plants which were located deep in Germany. It was a hectic week of escort for the 354th Fighter Group that went like this:

20th February: Escort to Brunswick. Bombers were contacted and Group Leader was informed that they were under attack and had no protection. No friendly fighters were seen when rendezvous was made. Fifty plus single-engine and several twin-engine fighters seen from rendezvous to target. Sixteen enemy aircraft were destroyed with no losses.

21st February: Escort to Brunswick. One squadron dispatched to take care of enemy fighters which engaged the group in the vicinity of Steinhuder Lake prior to rendezvous. Me 109s, FW 190s, Ju 88s, Me 110s and Me 210s seen in large numbers between rendezvous and target. 200 plus enemy aircraft seen by group. Left bombers in the vicinity of Osnabruck at 1445 hours. Ten enemy aircraft destroyed for the loss of two P-51s.

22nd February: Escort to Oscherseben and Halberstadt. Immediately after rendezvous twenty plus Me 110s escorted by thirty Me 109s encountered. Later between rendezvous and target eight Me 110s, five Ju 88s, eighteen FW 190s, and six Me 109s encountered. Four FW 190s and one Me 109 seen in target area. Thirteen enemy aircraft destroyed. Lost one P-51 which blew up in mid-air.

24th February: Escort to Schweinfurt. One squadron was continually distrupted by P-47s which continually made threatening advances. Encountered a few Focke Wulf 190s and

Further gun camera shots show the fatal moment in the pursuit of a Ju 88

Me 109s in vicinity of Lochen which were disbursed. One Me 210 shared with an unidentified P-38 the only victory of the day. No losses.

25th February: Escort to Nuremburg. Approximately ten Me 109s and ten FW 190s seen, most of these just west of Kitzingen. Lone Me 109 destroyed over the target. Seven victories in all. No losses.

After the tremendous aerial encounters of the first days of 'Big Week' it became apparent that the Luftwaffe was taking a beating in the air from the Mustangs regardless of the results of the bombing of the German aircraft plants. Of course, the Thunderbolts were still carrying the brunt of the escort duties and their toll during 'Big Week' was very high. The bombing raids on the German aircraft industry did not have the desired results and enemy fighter production continued to grow rather than decrease after 'Big Week'. What did happen was that the cream of the Luftwaffe was being destroyed in the gigantic air battles that were taking place. The fighting 'know-how' and skill of these veteran German pilots was something that could not be manufactured.

Following the initial appearance of the Mustangs over Berlin, the Eighth Air Force was eager for the weather to permit the bombers to attack the capital of the Third Reich in force. This was accomplished on 6th March, and while the weather was still very bad, a fifteen-mile-long parade of Fortresses and B-24 Liberators headed for the target and the Luftwaffe came up in force. Due to cloud cover the bombers deposited most of their explosives on a five mile stretch of Berlin's suburbs and none of them managed to hit their primary targets.

However this mission resulted in what was one of the greatest air battles of the Second World War. The Luftwaffe hit the oncoming raiders with 169 fighters on the way in, 202 over the target and 244 fighters on the way home. 615 P-47s, eighty-six P-38s and 102 P-51 were in the air that day to protect the 'Big Friends', but the bombers still lost sixty-nine of their number while eleven fighters failed to return to base.

While some bomb groups did not even see enemy fighters others were all but annihilated that day. Under particularly heavy attack were the B-17s of the 3rd Bomb Division who recorded that 'The enemy's method of attack against this division was skilfully executed. From both the offensive standpoint of the enemy fighters, and from the escort standpoint of our fighters, the bombers presented a column of combat wing pairs, covering from head to tail a distance of perhaps as much as sixty miles. The enemy controller, apparently having detected a gap in fighter escort in the center of the column, dispatched out of his concentration two formations of fighters to harrass the front end and the rear end of the column and to occupy the attention of the escort fighters at those two positions. Then he slammed his remaining 100 plus fighters against the momentarily unprotected center of the column. Working against time and with unusual aggressiveness, these fighters reaped a harvest of perhaps as many as twenty bombers during a period of less than thirty minutes.'

There were three groups of P-51s in the air that day. The 4th Fighter Group flying their new Mustangs, the veteran 354th 'Pioneer Mustang' Group and the relatively green 357th Group. In its first real air battle the 357th turned in a brilliant performance in downing twenty enemy planes without suffering a single loss of their own.

Major T L Hayes, Jr, took over the lead of the group after Lieutenant-Colonel Graham was forced to return to base with engine trouble. Rendezvous was effected with the bombers at 26,000 feet over Berlin. Several flights escorted each box of Fortresses over the target as they arrived.

At the same time other Mustangs of the unit had driven some forty enemy fighters down below the bombers and engaged them in combat. No other friendly fighters had been observed in the target area at the time of arrival of the first bombers. Some P-38s were seen fifty miles west of Berlin on withdrawal. When the last box of B-24s passed over the target the Mustangs of the 357th went with them some forty miles from Berlin where they left them to be picked up by the withdrawal force. On the way home the Mustangs dropped down on an airfield at Ulzen where one flight proceeded to strafe the field where four enemy aircraft were destroyed.

The P-51s of the 4th Group were also heavily engaged that day and claimed fifteen victories. One of the pilots who managed to bring down an enemy fighter and also get a good view of Berlin was Lieutenant Pierce McKennon. His combat report reads as follows:

'I was flying Green 3 in Greenbelt. The section was climbing to get some smoke trails at 1 o'clock to the bombers. When from the port side we saw about 50 plus coming in on the bombers. We jettisoned our wing tanks and started diving on them. From then on our section was split. An Me 109 came over me about 500 feet and started turning toward me. I pulled up in a steep turn and got on his tail. He started diving and I followed giving him a short burst.

One of the classic fighters of the Second World War, the North American P-51 Mustang was originally designed for the RAF, but was so successful, especially when the design was married to a Merlin engine, that it was adopted by the USAF also. Used in a multitude of roles, it found a special niche for itself in that of a long range escort fighter. Specification for P-51B Mustang: *Engine:* Packard V-1650 Merlin 1,620hp. *Armament:* Four .5-inch Browning machine guns (as escort). *Maximum speed:* 440mph at 30,000 feet. *Climb rate:* 3.6 minutes to 10,000 feet. *Maximum range:* 2,200 miles. *Ceiling:* 42,000 feet. *Weights empty/loaded:* 6,840/11,200 pounds. *Span:* 37 feet 0¼ inch. *Length:* 32 feet 3 inches

Personalized Mustangs supply a note of light relief in the serious business of war

I got strikes on the cockpit, engine and wing roots. He started smoking rather badly going toward Berlin. I got a dead line astern shot and got in some more strikes. He led me right down over the airdrome which was Templehof. I have never seen so many German aircraft as I saw there. They were in the circuit and some taking off. I followed this guy right over the drome and gave him another short burst when making a port turn. I was at about 500 feet in this port turn when he flicked on his back, went in and exploded over at one end of the airdrome. I pulled up and started after another 109 but due to oil over my windscreen he got away.'

Lieutenant Nicholas Megura won his first victories that day as Messerschmitt Me 110s lined up on the bombers to fire their rockets into them. Once under attack from Megura three of the 110s went into a dive with 'Cowboy' right behind them. Out of the corner of his eye Megura sighted what he thought was a Me 109 escorting the German twin-engined fighters bearing down upon him.

Immediately he broke off and turned into the oncoming fighter. To his relief, it proved to be another Mustang, so away he went after three more Me 110s who were lobbing their rockets into the bomber formation. He raked one with a long burst. The Messerschmitt went into a steep bank and disappeared into the clouds.

Another P-51 sized up the situation and formed up on Megura's wing. Now he could concentrate on the German fighter. A long burst directly on the tail of the Messerschmitt exploded it. Megura then fired into the wing and engine. The wing snapped off and tumbled to earth where it exploded. Megura now lined up on the belly tank of a Focke Wulf 190. He could just imagine it going up in flames as he pressed the gun button. Yet, nothing happened. He was out of ammunition. Breaking off the combat, he set course for England.

The 354th Group encountered some

fifty single-engined fighters just after rendezvous, but the Germans refused to fight with them and broke down into the clouds. All in all, the three groups of P-51s accounted for forty-one of the enemy that day. This made up over half of the claims for over 700 escorting fighters of the VIII Fighter Command. Truly it was a great day for the Mustangs.

One of the most famous 'teams' that was to fly with VIII Fighter Command was that of Don Gentile and Johnny Godfrey. These two really began to operate as a team on the next mission to Berlin on 8th March, 1944.

The Luftwaffe began to hit the bombers on the outskirts of Berlin. At that moment Godfrey and Gentile sighted some twenty German fighters ripping into one of the boxes of bombers head-on. They picked out five Messerschmitt 109s and the fight was on.

Godfrey was first to maneuver onto the tail of one of the Germans with Gentile covering. Short bursts got good strikes and Godfrey continued to fire into the enemy fighter until he rolled over on his back and the pilot bailed out.

Now it was Gentile's turn. He scored a direct hit on the tail of one 109, then, using combat flaps for tighter turns, the Mustang pilot gave a second enemy craft a burst of lead from 100 yards. The cockpit of the German fighter filled with smoke and the pilot went over the side.

Now there were German fighters all over the sky desperately trying to fight the escorting Mustangs and attack the bombers at the same time. Gentile and Godfrey sighted another pair of 109s attacking the bombers and headed for them. Strangely, the enemy fighters took no evasive action and the two American pilots opened fire simultaneously. Gentile's 109 rolled to the left and went down in flames. Godfrey's rolled to the right and went down burning. Already five down between the two of them.

The two Mustangs pulled back up to

4th Fighter Group P-51 ace Don Gentile with 'Shangri La'

22,000 feet to help the bombers out once more when they were intercepted by an Me 109 coming in from 4 o'clock. Both pilots broke into the German head-on and they flashed past each other.

As they circled, the three aircraft lined up for another head-on pass at each other. However, this time during the pass Gentile broke to the right and Godfrey to the left. Hauling hard back on the stick both Mustangs climbed and came roaring down on the tail of the German. In vain the 109 tried to outdive the P-51s but steadily they gained on him. Godfrey finally got in a good burst that showed strikes just before the 109 pulled out at approximately 500 feet.

The German plane had just begun to smoke when Godfrey ran out of ammunition. He slid over while Gentile pulled in behind him just above the treetops. Another burst and the Me 109 pilot pulled up to about 1,000 feet and bailed out. This made number six between the two.

Still their day was not over. On the way home they sighted a crippled B-17 straggling all alone. German fighters were lining above him like vultures for the kill. Although Godfrey was out of ammunition and Gentile was down to a bare minimum they slid in over the Fortress and began their criss-cross protective pattern. This was enough to discourage the Luftwaffe pilots. The 'Big Friend' lumbered on toward home with the bluffing Mustang pilots orbiting overhead.

The long range of the Mustangs brought about a change in tactics for German air controllers. When the entire VIII Bomber Command was committed the German fighters were dispatched to those points where it was known that the Mustangs would have to be leaving the formation and that would be out of range of the P-47s. This difficulty was rectified as

quickly as possible by converting some of the old veteran groups to Mustangs and initiating new units into combat. Former P-47 Groups converting to the Mustang in April of 1944 were the 355th, 352nd and 359th. The new 339th Fighter Group equipped with P-51s also entered combat that month.

The veteran 354th Fighter Group continued to escort the bombers deep into Germany and decimate formations of intercepting fighters that decided the odds were in their favor. On 16th March 1944, some thirty-five Me 109s, FW 190s and Me 110s made a concentrated effort against the bombers just outside the target at Augsburg. A simultaneous attack was made from all angles firing cannon all the way. P-51s of the 'Pioneer Mustangs' broke the attack up and downed ten of the enemy fighters.

On 8th April the 354th once more caught the fighters as some sixty FW 190s and fifteen Me 109s attacked the Brunswick-bound bombers in the vicinity of Wittigen. When the enemy aircraft made their first pass on the bombers three of the B-17s were seen to explode and three others were sent spinning out of formation. The sky was full of parachutes.

The Mustangs tore into their formations and when the fight was broken off fourteen Focke Wulf 190s and seven Me 109s had fallen to their guns. 'High scorers' for the day were Captains Don Beerbower and Jack T Bradley with three apiece. Four P-51s of the group did not make it home that day.

From this time, the Luftwaffe was beginning to pull its forces into Germany more and more in a vain effort to protect the vital targets of the Fatherland. This was the beginning of their conservation of fighter forces and the initiation of a phenomenon that the Allies were never able to understand – their withdrawal deeper

A 'Big Friend', with two escorting 'checkertails' of 325th Fighter Group in the background

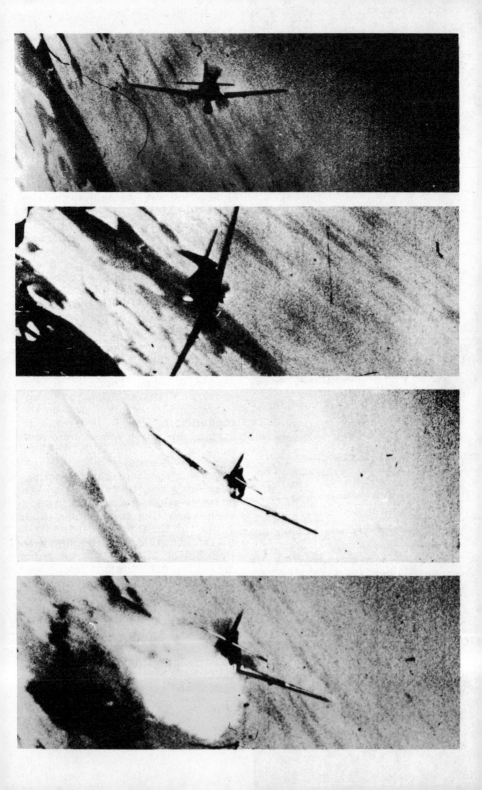

into Germany. Had the Luftwaffe intercepted the Allied fighters at the coast when they were laden with drop tanks they would have been forced to salvo these tanks before entering combat. This would have prevented the escort from going on to the target with the bombers. Fortunately, the Germans never changed their tactics but pulled further and further into Germany as the war progressed.

The selective interception of the

Another success in combat with an Fw 190

A formation of the 354th Group over France displaying invasion stripes on wings and fuselages

Luftwaffe changed a long standing tactic with VIII Fighter Command. It was only after the Berlin missions that the American fighters had begun to leave the bombers for a bit and strafe the German airfields on their way home. At the beginning of April 1944 the fighters were given permission by General Kepner to go down after the Luftwaffe rather than wait for it to come up to fight.

69

Strafing
and shuttles

The abundance of fighter groups available by April 1944 was a primary factor influencing General Kepner in his decision to allow his fighters to 'go low level'. When escort had been initiated the number of fighters, particularly P-51s, had been drastically limited and once fighters were available to go all the way with the bombers it had been hoped that the striking force would be sufficient to bring the Luftwaffe up to intercept each mission. In this manner, through the action of the fighters and combined firepower of massive bombers formations, the German fighter force would soon be depleted. When this failed the fighters went 'down to earth'.

Strangely enough, after its initial success as an escort fighter in the air, one of the roles of the P-51 reverted to that of its early sister, the A-36 Invader. The Mustang became a strafing craft once more. Through photo-Intelligence the German primary airfields and auxiliaries were located and mapped. But the vast majority of Luftwaffe airfields were well defended with flak guns of all calibers. As strafing attacks increased, defenses increased. These low level missions would cost the American fighter units many more casualties than they would suffer in the air.

General Kepner; at last his fighters are allowed to 'go low', taking the offensive to enemy airfields and other installations

About this time the new P-51D began to arrive in the theater. This was the Mustang with the famous 'bubble canopy' which was a tremendous improvement over the limited visibility from the 'greenhouse' of the P-51B. As a matter of fact, many of the P-51Bs had adopted the British-built 'Malcolm hood,' named after the designer of this clear plexiglass canopy. Visibility was excellent with the Malcolm hood and some of the Mustang pilots actually preferred it to the new bubble canopy on the P-51D'.

The P-51D also eliminated the gun jamming problem that had been experienced on the P-51B and added another .50 caliber machine gun in each wing to give the Mustang added firepower. About this time the 108-

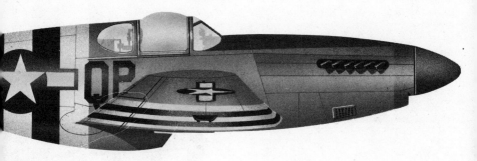

The North American P-51B was notable for two modifications: it was the first Mustang to be fitted with a Merlin engine, with which the Mustang came into its own as an all purpose fighter, and it was the first to be fitted with an improved, but not definitive cockpit canopy. The first Merlin conversions were undertaken by Rolls-Royce in England, but modifications to suit the Mustang for the Packard-built Merlin were also under way in the United States. The extra power of the Merlin necessitated the strengthening of the airframe and the provision of a four-bladed propeller, but the effort and time required for this were handsomely repaid in the Mustang's enhanced performance, especially at altitude. The first conversions to an improved canopy were again undertaken in the United Kingdom, when a specially-designed bulged hood (the Malcolm hood, as in the illustrations) was fitted to RAF and some USAAF machines. This modification was a great improvement over the earlier canopy, but it was not adopted on the production lines as the new and even better bubble canopy was on the way. The first P-51Bs to reach an active theatre arrived in Britain in December 1943 and went into action later that month. *Engine:* Packard V-1650-3 Merlin, 1,450hp at 19,800 feet. *Armament:* Four Browning MG 53-2 machine guns with 350 rounds (inner pair) and 280 rounds (outer pair) per gun, plus two 1,000-lb bombs. *Speed:* 440mph at 30,000 feet. *Climb:* 7 minutes to 20,000 feet. *Ceiling:* 42,000 feet. *Range:* 550 miles clean and 2,200 miles maximum with drop tanks. *Weight empty/loaded:* 6,840/11,200lbs. *Span:* 37 feet 0¼ inches. *Length:* 32 feet 3 inches. *Role:* Interceptor fighter, long range escort fighter or fighter-bomber. The fitting of the Merlin engine meant that the nose had to be redesigned to place the carburettor air intake below the nose instead of above it as on the Allison-engined models

A total of 14,819 Mustangs was constructed in the United States, and in the European theatre US Mustangs flew 213,873 missions, dropping 5,668 tons of bombs and destroying 4,950 enemy aircraft in the air and 4,131 on the ground for a loss to themselves of 2,520

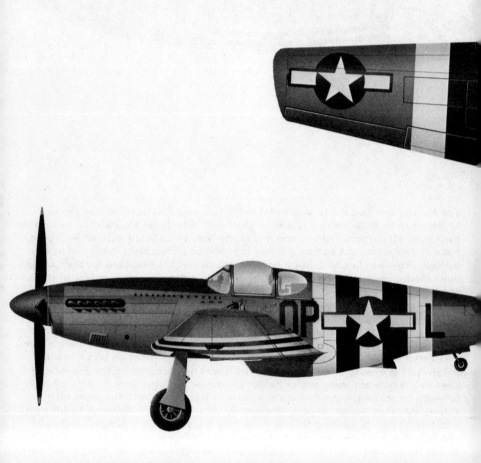

P-51Ds had the all-round-view bubble canopy and other improvements; English mud and slush still presented problems, however

gallon drop tank became available in quantity giving the Mustang a range of 850 miles. The P-51 had become a formidable weapon.

Early strafing mission tactics were more often than not left to the discretion of the combat leader. The initial efforts were usually made while returning from escorting the bombers and were more a case of taking advantage of surprise against these targets of opportunity than being formally planned.

One of the early planned strafing attacks is described by Lieutenant Thomas Biel of the 4th Fighter Group:

'At 1500 hours "Upper" called to say that he was letting down and for us to look for our target. We made a port turn on the deck when "Upper" called and said he was attacking an airdrome, which I believe was north-west of

Brandenberg. Pectin Squadron circled around a lake near the drome for about ten minutes when Pectin Leader called and said he was going to attack the same airdrome.

'Approaching the Brandenberg/Briest airfield, I saw at least ten aircraft burning. I picked out a Heinkel III near the hangers. I observed many hits on this aircraft and when closing in and still firing, the HeIII burst into flame.

'I was concentrating on my HeIII and was unable to observe results of Captain Beeson's and Lieutenant Carr's attack on the aircraft in the center of the field.

'Pectin White Section then made a starboard turn and started to head west on the deck. Moderate flak was being thrown up at us. A few minutes later I saw ahead of me a motor barge towing three other barges. I depressed my nose and started to fire. I observed many hits on the motor barge. It burst into a cloud of smoke.

'We saw a Greenbelt pilot (Call name

for another squadron) attacking a Ju
88 in the air. He called up and said for
us to finish off the enemy aircraft because he was out of ammo. Immediately, Captain Beeson and I closed in on
the Ju 88 whose left engine was smoking. I saw Captain Beeson get hits on
the Ju 88 and then pull away. I cut my
throttle and closed in to about 250
yards and began to fire, getting hits all
over his cockpit and right engine. I
kept firing until the Ju 88 crashed on a
field and burst into flames. I came
back and took a picture of the burning
Ju 88. I claim this one shared with
Lieutenant Fielder of the 335th Squadron and Captain Beeson.

'Captain Beeson, Pectin Leader,
then called to say he was setting a
course of 274 and climbing up. After
flying in that direction for about
eight minutes, Pectin Leader called to
say he was going down on an airdrome
at nine o'clock to us. I broke down
with him and his No 2 man, Lieutenant
Carr, from about 3,000 feet and when
approaching the airdrome, I saw about
ten Ju 88s in perfect alignment facing
us.

'I saw Captain Beeson clobbering the
the first Ju 88, setting it on fire and
then shooting up the other nine. I confirm the Ju 88 for Captain Beeson. I
also saw Lieutenant Carr knocking
pieces off the second Ju 88 and then
strafing the other eight Ju 88s. I confirm one Ju 88 destroyed by Lieutenant
Carr.

'I got hits on the remaining five or
six Ju 88s, and I concentrated on the
last Ju 88 observing hits all over and
smoke pouring out. I at first claimed
this one destroyed but later changed
it to a probable.

'While this was going on, the Germans were throwing up intense flak

**108-gallon drop tanks allowed
Mustangs to operate anywhere in
Germany**

Strafing of air fields is intensified and the Luftwaffe's losses soar

which was very accurate. I first saw Captain Beeson get hit and glycol streaming out and then his No 2, Lieutenant Carr, got hit and his glycol began to stream. I got hit in the fuselage and tail unit. I heard Lieutenant Carr say that he was hit. I did not see him bail out. Captain Beeson called to say he would have to bail out shortly. Evading on the deck, I set course and came home'.

The date of this mission was 5th April 1944 and the Captain Beeson mentioned was one of the top fighter aces in Europe at the time. He was credited with nineteen victories in the air and had seven strafing credits before falling to flak on that mission. The coolant system of the Mustang made it very susceptible to ground fire and Beeson was one of many who was lost through its vulnerability.

The actual target of this mission had been the airfield at Jüteborg, but weather conditions did not permit the 4th Group to locate it. Group Commander Don Blakeslee had wisely had his Intelligence Officer brief the Mustang pilots on the airdromes at Brandenburg/Briest, Brandenburg/Industriehafen, Weissewarte, Buch and Stendal, none of which were more than forty miles from Berlin and all the targets were attacked.

Blakeslee credited the tremendous success of destroying forty-five aircraft on the ground and damaging forty-nine others to the element of surprise. As he put it, 'These airdromes were well inland and at that phase of the war the Germans must have felt rather secure in there. They had never been strafed before; perhaps they never expected to be. At any rate they were surprised completely. At Stendal, there was no flak at all on our first three passes and only meager flak on our fourth. There we destroyed

Gun camera photographs show the success of ground-level strikes

twenty-three German aircraft and damaged fourteen more.

Within a few weeks the Germans had strengthened the defenses of the airdromes to the extent that the Mustangs had to plan very carefully to come across for only one pass on the airdromes. Once alerted, the flak was concentrated enough to decimate flights attempting subsequent strafing runs.

During the month of April 1944 VIII Fighter Command destroyed 493 enemy aircraft and damaged another 455 on the ground. Its fighter pilots also came to the realisation of the tremendous price they had to pay. While only one out of each hundred fighters dispatched in support of the bombers was lost, three out of each hundred fighters attacking ground targets were lost during April and May of 1944.

Spring 1944 also saw the England-based Mustangs begin dive bombing attacks. The usual bomb load on the P-51 was a 500-pounder slung under each wing. These were primarily used against bridges, roads and rail targets prior to the impending invasion of the Continent. Most of the pilots who were attacking transportation preferred to go after locomotives. Pilots were still warned against strafing passenger trains in occupied countries but if they could get a clear shot at the engine this would be permissable. However, most of the trains strafed were freights which were usually laden with war supplies.

Another inovation the Mustang pilots employed against ground targets was the use of drop tanks. The P-51s would dive down in string formation and release their partially full tanks on the target. Once it had been saturated in gasoline they would go back and fire their guns into the inflammable area and everything in the vicinity would go up in flames. This method was quite effective on a train carrying munitions or military equipment once the locomotive had been put out of commission.

From spring 1944 until the end of the war in Europe the Mustang pilots would continue to bomb and strafe the German airdromes and lines of communication and supply on the ground. Yet, the greatest job went on – that of getting the bombers to the target and keeping the Luftwaffe fighters from getting to the 'Big Friends'.

As the Mustangs continued to take the 'heavies' to targets deeper and deeper inside Germany day after day the weight of numbers began to break the back of the Luftwaffe fighter forces. Many veteran German pilots fell under the guns of the Americans, and young men fresh out of flying school were pressed into the ranks. In many cases, these pilots had not had the time to be sufficiently trained in the art of combat to properly contest the ability of the Mustang pilots. A sign of dire times to come for the constantly harrassed German pilots was related after a mission on 8th May 1944, by Lieutenant John F Thornell of the 352nd Fighter Group.

'I joined up with White Leader, 487th Fighter Squadron of our Group. We spotted three Me 109s drawing contrails heading for the bombers. They broke for the deck and we followed. I was in the lead on the bounce.

'At 50-110 yards range I opened fire on the No 2 man in the enemy formation. He burst into flames and hit the ground. I was down to 2,000 feet by then. I then slid over and fired at the No 1 enemy aircraft. He fell apart in the air and the fuselage hit the ground and exploded.

'We started for home but I lost 487th Squadron Leader (Lt-Col John C Meyer) in the clouds. When I was at 3,000 feet I observed an Me 109 on my tail. Thinking I was out of ammunition I called to Colonel Meyer but he couldn't find me. I was turning with this Me 109 at this time. Colonel Meyer called and said to chew his tail off because I was close enough. As I turned inside the enemy aircraft, I

Mustang pilot John C Meyer in his considerably decorated airplane

Above: P-51s of 355th Group blast Me 110s. *Below:* D-Day markings on 9th Air Force Mustangs

closed to ten or fifteen yards when he immediately bailed out.

'I dropped below the clouds and saw his chute open and saw him land in the woods.'

As the air war over Europe progressed, American pilots would witness many occasions when the untried, insufficiently trained Luftwaffe pilots would go over the side as soon as they got a Mustang on their tail.

By the end of May vast armadas of Allied aircraft were daily pounding the French coast. Railroads, marshalling yards, roads, bridges, and lines of communication were under constant attack in preparation for the invasion of the continent of Europe. D-Day was imminent.

After several alerts the final word was given on the evening of 5th June, 1944. All unofficial communications between the airbases and the outside were cut off. Group Commanders reported to General Kepner, Commander of VIII Fighter Command, that evening for instruction. On arrival they were given the news: the invasion would begin the following day.

The P-51s were fuelled, armed and loaded with 500-lb bombs that night. Broad black and white stripes were painted on the wings and around the fuselage for identification purposes. Throughout the night the roar of aircraft was constant as bombers headed inland for their targets and transport aircraft loaded with paratroops and towing gliders headed for the Normandy Peninsula to deposit the vanguard of the invasion troops.

At 0300 hours the fighter pilots slipped into their cockpits and taxied out into the darkness. Roaring down the runways, one after the other, the Mustangs of the Eighth and Ninth Air Forces rose into the cloudy skies to form up in the 3,000-airplane armada that would provide the greatest aerial umbrella the world had ever known.

The Ninth Air Force fighters maintained top cover over the invasion area while the fighters of the Eighth Air Force headed further inland to sweep the area clear of any Luftwaffe craft that dared to venture into the invasion area.

To the amazement of many Allied leaders, but to the chagrin of many of the fighter pilots, the German Air Force did not challenge the invasion beaches that morning. *Oberst* Hans Priller and his wingman were the only members of the Luftwaffe fighter unit JG26 still based in France when the landings were made as the rest of their aircraft had just been pulled into Germany. Priller was ordered to challenge the vast armada and this he did in one screaming, strafing pass. After that the beachheads were free of attack the rest of the morning.

The Mustangs that went inland found plenty of action bombing and strafing. Other P-51 pilots caught enemy aircraft trying to break through the aerial armada. Captain Shel Monroe of the 4th Fighter Group chased an FW 190 all over Paris before he finally brought it down.

Mission after mission was mounted that day as the fighters relentlessly struck at German transport. The inability of the enemy to bring reinforcements to the front on D-Day and the days immediately following it played a great part in the success of the Allied victory on the Normandy beaches.

The Mustang pilots looked forward to the day when they could get the Luftwaffe back in the sky to challenge them once more. The spirits of the pilots of the 4th Fighter Group were lifted when they began to hear rumors of a highly classified mission that was coming up. Speculation as to the type and destination of the operation created a great deal of excitement amongst the entire unit.

The orders were received on 21st June. The 4th Fighter Group reinforced by the 486th Fighter Squadron of the 352nd Fighter Group had been picked to escort three combat wings of 144 B-17s on the first shuttle mission to Russia. Ground crews of the bomb groups had been sent to prepare bases

The fighter in its bomber guise

at Poltava, Morgorod and Piryatin some months before. The idea of the shuttle mission was both to illustrate to the Germans that the Americans could mount bombing missions back and forth across their country at will and to create a favorable effect of cooperation with the Russians.

The mission was expected to take the escorting Mustangs seven and a half hours to complete which was not an extraordinary chore for the aircraft, but Colonel Don Blakeslee impressed upon his pilots before departure that they were not to drop their tanks under any circumstances until they were empty. To do so would prevent them from reaching Russia.

At 0728 hours the seventy P-51s were airborne and became a part of the 12th mission to Berlin. In an enormous show of airpower 1,374 B-17s and B-24s escorted by twenty-six fighter groups of the Eight and Ninth Air Forces headed for their targets. The 4th

Group crossed the enemy coast north of Overflakke Island at 20,000 feet and proceeded to fly across a cloud-blanketed Germany. Rendezvous was made with the bombers at Leszno, Poland, where the Mustangs jettisoned their empty fuel tanks.

Approximately an hour and a half later some twenty black-nosed Me 109s attacked the formation near Diedice, Poland. Five of them were downed by the Mustangs, but one P-51 was lost along with one of the bombers.

Once the action had been broken the Mustangs continued on into Russia. The bombers broke off to go into their base at Poltava while the P-51s proceeded toward their destination at Piryatin. Blakeslee began to check his watch and fuel gauges apprehensively as the 1,600 mile flight neared its end. Suddenly a volley of flares appeared. The fighters had hit their base right

Equipped for long-range escort duty a Mustang takes off from a steel-matting airfield in Italy

A P-51D with rocket-launching tubes

on the head and within a minute or so of their estimated time of arrival.

That night a great and jubilant banquet was given in honor of the Mustang pilots. Vodka flowed freely and toast after toast was made far into the night.

The second night proved to be a nightmare. A German bomber had followed the formation of Americans on the previous day and pinpointed the Russian bases on which the Fortresses and Mustangs had landed. With this knowledge, the Luftwaffe mounted a large mission the second night that the men were in Russia. The hardest hit target was the airfield at Poltava where a large percentage of the bombers were destroyed.

However, the Mustangs were not

the P-51s landed at Lucrera airfield near Foggia.

On 2nd July the Eighth Air Force Mustangs went on an escort mission with the Fifteenth Air Force to Budapest. The 4th Fighter Group experienced difficulties from the beginning of this mission. Their P-51s were not equipped with dust filters which were necessary in the Mediterranean, and also the nozzles of the belly tanks were of different size which caused an insufficient flow of fuel to the engines. By the time the fighters reached the target the 4th was closer to the size of a squadron than a group.

Colonel Don Blakeslee was leading what was left of his unit over the target area when some sixty Messerschmitt 109s were sighted heading for the bombers. The Mustangs roared down to the attack and caught the formation of German fighters from the rear. Four of the Luftwaffe fighters went spinning down from the first pass.

Major Howard 'Deacon' Hively got on the tail of a 109 and started blasting away, but immediately discovered that he had an enemy fighter on his own tail. As the 109 exploded, Hively took a cannon shell in his canopy. Plexiglass went all over the cockpit and blood from his cuts blinded Hively in one eye. Disregarding his injury, he tore back into the enemy formation and shot two more of them from the sky before he broke off the combat.

On 5th July the Eighth Air Force P-51s left Italy and escorted the bombers to rail targets over France before continuing on to England. The round-robin shuffle mission was one of the greatest triumphs of long range escort flying even though the Mustangs had managed to down only fifteen enemy aircraft. The impression that the flight had made on the German High Command was sufficient. The enemy could never know from which direction he would be hit and in what force. The Mustang had shown that it could take the bombers with impunity anywhere they wanted.

overlooked. A number of Junkers Ju 88s arrived and bombed and strafed the airfield. Four Mustangs of the 4th Fighter Group managed to take to the air, but their attempt at interception was futile.

The following day the Mustangs escorted the remnants of the bombers down to Italy. The bombers hit an oil refinery in Poland on the way. The mission was largely uneventful and

Europe – the final battles

Summer 1944 saw the Mustangs ranging all over Europe. They went after the Luftwaffe in the air on escort missions and fighter sweeps, and on the ground in strafing missions.

Lieutenant Sherman Armsby of the 361st Fighter Group attacked a formation of some thirty enemy aircraft. The Messerschmitts' formation was broken up and the Mustangs showed their diving ability by chasing them to the deck as they took evasive action.

Armsby caught one of them and sent him down in flames. 'The lead Me 109 then took out across country on the deck about 1,000 yards in front of me,' recounted Armsby. 'I pulled up flaps and started after him. I followed him for ten minutes through trees, power lines and every other ground obstacle he could find. I fired intermittently but got few hits due to his violent evasive actions. As I pulled up directly behind him my ammunition gave out so I called White Four to close up and

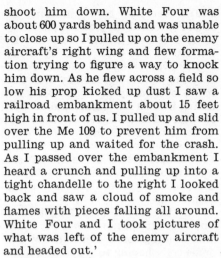

shoot him down. White Four was about 600 yards behind and was unable to close up so I pulled up on the enemy aircraft's right wing and flew formation trying to figure a way to knock him down. As he flew across a field so low his prop kicked up dust I saw a railroad embankment about 15 feet high in front of us. I pulled up and slid over the Me 109 to prevent him from pulling up and waited for the crash. As I passed over the embankment I heard a crunch and pulling up into a tight chandelle to the right I looked back and saw a cloud of smoke and flames with pieces falling all around. White Four and I took pictures of what was left of the enemy aircraft and headed out.'

The performance of the Mustang enabled it to outdive or outclimb any aircraft it encountered over Europe except the German jets which began to appear in summer 1944. Even the long-nosed Focke Wulf 190D was not able to stay with the P-51 with an experienced pilot in the cockcpit, as is witnessed by the performance of Lieutenant Robert O Peters on a mission to Leipzig on 20th July 1944.

'I spotted a long nose FW 190 hitting a B-17 already on fire all along the port wing. I turned sharply to catch him and my wingman spun, losing me. I closed to about 400 yards and gave him a burst. The B-17 had rolled over on its back and was starting down. Hits were observed on the cowl and cockpit of the Focke Wulf 190. He jinked and started violent evasive action finally splitessing for the deck from 21,000 feet. I firewalled everything and started after him. He took such violent evasive action that it surprised me that the plane held together. I fired one or two bursts going down and then hit compressibility. A burst from my gun helped me recover. Another burst hit his cockpit. He jettisoned it and bailed out a few seconds later at

Some of the many hundreds of Mustangs which came into service in the final stages of the war

3-5,000 feet just barely missing my ship. I watched his plane explode.

'As I started down I saw another FW 190 on the deck close by. I firewalled everything and had no trouble catching up. He apparently didn't see me. I opened up at about 300 yards seeing hits on his engine and cockpit. He started a 46-degree banking turn to the left. After 180 degrees I gave him another burst that went square into the cockpit. He rolled on his left side and exploded in a farmer's back yard. I made two camera passes for confirmation.

'On the second pass I spotted an airfield on to the north that the FW 190 was heading for. I came in low over some trees hoping to get some FW 190s lined up on the west side. I miscalculated and came in on the east side. A Ju 88 and He 111 were in front of me and I fired at the He 111 observing hits on the left wing, motor and fuselage, setting the plane on fire. I continued on past the field and made a 180-degree turn behind a hill and came in for the FW 190s again. I missed position and took the Ju 88 under a camouflage netting. I observed hits on the left engine but am not sure that I destroyed it at this time. I received no flak on either pass and was determined to hit the FW 190s so I turned for another pass.

'At this time I spotted a Dornier 217 on the trees just after takeoff. I moved into position about 500 yards behind him and opened up as he entered a left turn. I fired three bursts observing hits on the left wing, engine and fuselage, starting the left engine smoking. He was making a turn back to the field and I got a few more hits on his left engine with one gun. The other three guns jammed. As we neared the field they put up intense 20mm flak and I swerved to avoid it. He went in and floated the width of the field finally forcing the plane down just short of the woods on the east edge of the field. As he hit, the left engine burst into flames and the left wing exploded near the root.

'For a second or two I had my head up and locked while looking at the field. A close burst of flak brought me out of it in time to see a long-nose 190 about 200 yards behind me blasting away. How he missed me I'll never know. I really panicked and started to climb. Then I hit for the deck, in a tight left turn. I completed a 360-degree turn about 20 feet off the deck and ended up close to his tail, as he didn't follow me. I was out of ammunition and had to pass him up. He scared me so that I probably would have missed him anyway. I put everything forwards and got out.'

Two aircraft destroyed in the air and three on the ground and still the Mustang escaped.

As the German Air Force took steady losses their experienced pilots began to diminish greatly in number. The young pilots that took to the air were often led by a few veterans and flew in large formations or 'gaggles' as the Mustang pilots began to call them. More often than not they did not break formation to challenge the American pilots, but bored in steadily towards the bomber formations until the P-51s slashed into them with guns blazing and broke them up. Even then some of the German pilots would hold formation doggedly until they were shot down.

Such a formation was encountered by the 532nd Fighter Group while escorting the bombers to Berlin on 6th August 1944. Major George Preddy turned in an outstanding performance on that mission.

A formation of some thirty Messerschmitt 109s headed into the third box of bombers from the rear of the bomber stream when Preddy took his flight into the fray. Jockeying his P-51 onto the tail of the nearest enemy fighter, he opened fire getting good strikes and the 109 went over on its back and spun down in flames.

Left with only his wingman, Lieutenant Heyer, Preddy quickly lined up on another 109, set him on fire and followed him down to 20,000 feet where the pilot bailed out. The enemy formation stayed together taking practically no evasive action and this allowed Preddy to line up on a third 109 which he promptly shot down.

At this time four more P-51s roared in to help in the destruction. The formation of Germans was still holding together so another burst from directly astern flamed number four which spiralled off to the right going down, but Preddy hung with them, hitting and burning number five. The enemy descended to 5,000 feet where one of them pulled off to the left. Preddy was now alone, so he took off after this plane to keep it from slipping in behind him. Round and round they went in tight turns until Preddy managed to turn inside of the German aircraft and come up on his tail. As he put a burst into the other plane the pilot bailed out.

George Preddy then headed back to base where he was met by his fellow pilots who were jubilant over his feat. When told he was credited with six

Above: Major George Preddy, credited with six kills (Bf 109s) when escorting bombers to Berlin, 6th August 1944
Below: Blue nosed P-51 of 352nd Group prepared for long distance mission

Weapons dropped to the fighters in Warsaw by Mustang-escorted bombers

enemy aircraft he could hardly believe it himself.

The Mustangs of the 355th Fighter Group flew a most unusual long range escort mission on 18th September 1944. Their P-51s escorted a wing of B-17s on a mission to carry supplies to the besieged Polish partisans in Warsaw. These patriots had risen against the Germans when they thought the Russian advance was close at hand. Unfortunately, the Russians did not come and the partisans were fighting for their lives within the city.

Major Daniel M Lewis, the Intelligence Officer of the 355th, went aboard one of the Flying Fortresses and told of the mission on his return:

"The City of Warsaw on the western bank of the coiling Vistula was visible for twenty minutes before we reached it. The surrounding country, from our altitude of 16,000 feet, appeared flat and rather unproductive, like some of the wastelands of our own far west. A thick layer of dust and smoke hung over the city, the sick breath of the war in its streets.

'Our Mustangs were weaving overhead as we began our run prepatory to dropping the supplies of guns, ammunition, food and medicine to the Polish patriots below. The lead group of bombers had already entered the range of the German heavy flak.

'We slid into our appointed dropping position in the force. As we got closer and closer to the city, occupied in part by the Germans while the Poles held other sections, the black puffs filled the sky. The next few seconds reminded me of the final approach to the top slope of the roller-coaster at the State Fair Park as the big ship lurched and swayed. For four or five minutes, we were in the thick of it as we weaved in evasive action, trying to dodge the bursting shells of ack-ack fire.

'As the bomb bay doors opened I thought for an instant of the hope in the visible faces looking up from below. What manna from heaven these bundles must be! I remembered the quotation in the British press, "Hang on – Relief is on the way".

'I glanced downwards. Drums, loaded with supplies of every kind, were floating earthward under blue, green and orange parachutes. The crews of several bombers destroyed by flak could be discerned by their white parachutes.

'I heard later that the enemy fighters had hovered about our fighters and bombers fifteen minutes before the target. Then, on the target run, the Me 109s came smashing through. Our fighters chased them into the flak. That was where we lost our two fighters.

'Instead of seeing the flash of guns and the movement of armies, soldiers, tanks and everything one associates with war on the ground, it seemed like a deserted city, as silent as a western ghost town.

'We turned eastwards, back over the Vistula and set course for our base beyond Poland, deep in the Ukraine. It was then about 1300 hours. We had been flying since 0530 and there were still four hours of flying ahead of us, but I looked forward to every minute of the remainder of the trip. It was a great relief to get out of the gun fire and away from the attacks of Me 109s which had been peppering us over the target without my knowing about it. I had not seen them but I had noticed the red bursts of flak which is often the signal for the fighters to hit the bombers.

'There were hundreds of evergreen forests dotting the Polish landscape and western Russia. As we penetrated further into Russia the same flat land continued, but the forests disappeared and gave way to great vistas of grain fields.

'This was the Russian breadbasket. It was comforting to think that the Russians had won it back. What a prize for the Germans to lose'.

The 354th 'Pioneer Mustang' Group of the Ninth Air Force went to France shortly after D-Day and flew many ground support missions and fighter sweeps for the onrushing Allied armoured and infantry columns.

Not only did this unit excel in bombing and strafing ground targets, but it continued to take its toll of German aircraft as it had done on the escort missions. Even on bombing missions the pilots of the 354th continued to demonstrate the superiority of their Mustangs over the enemy.

Captain Wallace N Emmer was on a dive-bombing mission over France on 12th June, 1944, when his formation was engaged by enemy aircraft. Immediately he turned into the attack on an oncoming Focke Wulf 190. Although he still had two 500-lb bombs slung under his wings he shot the aircraft from the sky. He then went on and bombed his target.

Narrow escapes were not unusual during those busy days of summer 1944. Lieutenant John S Miller of the 354th was hit over Cherbourg on 23rd July and had to leave his Mustang. After going over the side he suffered a tremendous blow and lost consciousness. He recovered to find himself hung on the horizontal stabiliser, the leading edge lodged in his belly. With both hands he flipped the leading edge over his head, fell clear of the P-51 and reached for the ripcord. It was not there and he spent anxious seconds locating it on his back where it had slipped. He then pulled the ripcord and floated down to earth where he was assisted by Allied ground troops.

The 354th suffered a tremendous blow on 9th August when it lost two of its leading aces, Major Don M Beerbower and Captain Wallace N Emmer. Beerbower led a sixteen-plane formation on an armed reconnaissance of the areas of Reims and Epernay. After making a pass on an airfield about three miles north of Reims, drawing intense flak and seeing thirty Junkers Ju 88s parked in revetments, Major Beerbower directed an attack in which he went in on the field from east to west as a diversion to draw flak, while the other Mustangs went in from north

Above: P-51s flying in close formation over England. *Below:* A Fw 190 unwise enough to stray into Allied air-space over Normandy

to south to hit the enemy aircraft.

Brazenly, he flew into the face of the flak installations in a diving attack, destroying a Ju 88 and knocking out two gun emplacements while effectively drawing the flak fire to himself. Beerbower was successful in drawing the fire away from his attacking formation, but he took hit after hit in his own Mustang. Desperately he pulled up in an attempt to gain enough altitude to bail out, but his attempt was in vain. He went over the side, but his parachute failed to open before he struck the ground.

Late the same afternoon, Captain Wallace Emmer led twelve Mustangs on the second armed reconnaissance mission of the day. Since that morning Emmer had been morose and silent. The loss of his close friend, Major Beerbower, undoubtedly affected him deeply. Had he not been ordered elsewhere, he might well have attempted to avenge the death of his fellow ace.

In an attack about five miles north of Rouen, while flying at 11,000 feet,

Rocket-powered Me 163s were too few and too unreliable to pose a real threat, despite phenomenal climb rate and high altitude performance

Emmer's Mustang took a flak hit which exploded and took large pieces off his aircraft. As his P-51 spun earthwards in flames, Emmer took to his parachute and drifted down to become a prisoner of war. Unfortunately, his burns proved fatal a few days later.

The first German jet encountered by the Americans was not really a jet-powered craft, but a rocket-powered small aircraft which used T-stoff (hydrogen peroxide and water) with C-stoff (hydrazine hydrate and methyl alcohol) as a catalyst for its engine. This tiny craft could climb to 30,000 feet in 2.6 minutes, but its endurance on power was limited to twelve minutes of actual fuel burnage. Its speed at altitude was 590 miles per hour, making it impossible for the Mustang or any other Allied piston-powered fighter to catch.

Above: Even the brilliantly designed Me 262 jet interceptor falls victim to the Mustang. *Below:* Another Me 262 about to be destroyed by a P-15. A Mustang's gun camera recorded this scene

The other German jet fighter was a much more formidable opponent. The Messerschmitt Me 262 was a pure twin jet powered with two Junkers Jumo axial-flow turbojet engines, each developing 1,980 pounds of static thrust. It was armed with four 30mm MK 108 cannon and had a speed of 538 miles per hour at 30,000 feet. This aircraft would have undoubtedly given the Allied bomber formations a very bad time had it been committed to combat earlier. However, Hitler saw fit to first commit the new jet as a bomber! Only at the insistence of members of the Luftwaffe high command late in 1944 did they convince him to allow the aircraft to be used in its originally designed role.

Lieutenant-Colonel John B Murphy of the 359th Fighter Group scored the first victory over an Me 163 on 16th August, 1944, when a number of the rocket-powered craft attacked a formation of B-17s in the vicinity of Leipzig. Murphy and his wingman caught one of the German fighters after it had made a pass at a crippled bomber and overshot its target. Both of the Mustang pilots scored hits on the Me 163 which escaped them by splitessing and diving for the deck.

Murphy then sighted another Me 163 some 5,000 feet below him and dived down to the attack. This craft was hoaded down and perhaps had expended all of its fuel for it made no attempt to speed away. Murphy caught it in the inside of a turn, opened fire at 700 feet and closed to a hundred feet, still firing at the German fighter. Hits on the left side of the fuselage set set off an explosion and the Me 163 tumbled earthwards to its destruction.

Regardless of the ability of the German jets, total Allied air superiority spelled doom for the majority of their operations. The long range of the Mustang made it possible for the P-51 pilots to orbit their bases for long periods of time in the hope that the German jets would attempt to take off. If they did get airborne, the P-51s would be there waiting for them when they came home to roost. Some Mustang units even planned extensive fighter sweeps and strafing missions to destroy the German jet menace on the ground. Top cover of Focke Wulf 190s and Messerschmitt 109s failed to rectify the situation.

The first Me 262 unit was headed by the famed 250-plus victory German ace, Major Walter Novotny. Some thirty aircraft were assigned to the unit, which was known as Kommando Novotny. Initial assignment of the aircraft was to airbases at Achmer and Hesepe near Osnabruck, Germany. With the initiation of this unit to combat jet encounters became more common.

While the new unit managed some success, it steadily lost its aircraft, primarily through accidents. With the crash program under which it was organised the pilots just did not have the time to become as proficient in the jets as would have been desired nor did the maintenance men have the time to eliminate the many 'bugs' which plagued the aircraft.

The final day of operations for the Kommando took place on 8th November 1944. On that day it lost four Me 262s including its famed commander, Major Novotny. He attacked a formation of bombers and then he in turn was attacked by a number of Mustangs. His final transmission was: 'Just made the third kill . . . left jot has failed . . . been attacked again . . . been hit'. His Me 262 crashed some six kilometers north of Bramsche before he could get out.

As the bombers ranged into Germany in autumn 1944 the Mustangs continued to tear into the Luftwaffe formations in what might be called the 'Battle of the Gaggles'. When the Luftwaffe did come up they came in force and many of the formations that headed for the bombers were in gaggles of forty to sixty aircraft.

Quite a number of pilots got five or more in one combat during November. Among those were two Eighth Air Force fighter aces from different

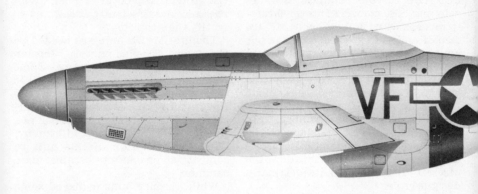

The North American P-51D was the first production model to have a bubble canopy and cut-down rear fuselage. It undertook the first US fighter strikes from land bases against Tokyo in April 1945 and in Western Europe was used principally as a high altitude escort aircraft. The first production models did not have the extra dorsal fin of later models, which was necessary to compensate for the reduced keel area of the cut-down fuselage. The last production models had two zero-length launching rails for 5-inch rockets. *Engine:* One Packard V-1650-7 Merlin inline, 1,695mph. *Armament:* Six Browning MG 53-2 .5-inch machine guns with 400 rounds (inner pair) and 270 rounds (outer two pairs) per gun, or four .5-inch machine guns with 400 rounds per gun, plus two 500- or 1,000-lb bombs or six 5-inch rockets. *Speed:* 437mph at 25,000 feet. *Climb:* 7.3 minutes to 20,000 feet. *Ceiling:* 41,900 feet. *Range:* 950 miles clean and 2,080 miles maximum with two 92-gallon drop tanks. *Weight empty/loaded:* 7,125 /12,100lbs. *Span:* 37 feet 0¼ inches. *Length:* 32 feet 3 inches. *Role:* Interceptor fighter, long range escort fighter or fighter-bomber

Bill Whisner – five victories (Fw 190s) in one mission

groups that fell in on one of the gaggles on an escort mission to Merseburg, Germany. Lieutenant Claude J Crenshaw of the 359th Fighter Group had become separated from his squadron in a layer of haze while escorting the bombers, so he and his wingman attacked a gaggle of German fighters alone. At about this time the formation was attacked by eight blue-nosed P-51s of the 352nd Fighter Group, one of whose flights was led by Captain William T Whisner.

Crenshaw immediately destroyed two of the 190s with both of the pilots bailing out The gaggle now turned to hit the bomber formation and Crenshaw followed one of them down through the bombers, peppering him all the way. As they broke through the heavies the 190 rolled over on its back and went down flaming.

Claude then recovered from his dive, climbed back up and encountered another gaggle of Focke Wulf 190s. From this formation he claimed a fourth victim before he had to break off the fight as a number of the 190s got on his tail.

In the meantime, Whisner had been

having a field day against the 190s. He fell in on the rear of a gaggle and hanging and skidding right in behind them, sent four down in flames. The fourth had gone into a steep right turn and in cutting him off and destroying him, Whisner had been pulled away from the main German formation.

Pushing his throttle to the firewall, he came back and caught another 190 in the layer of haze that seemed to hang about 29,000 feet. Whisner gave him a burst, but could not see any results due to the haze. Then the German snapped into a tight spin and went down, being recorded as a probable. Whisner then picked up another and blew him up for his fifth victory, with strikes on his belly tank. Amazingly enough, the German pilots had never bothered to jettison their belly tanks.

Crenshaw broke when the Germans got on his tail, and he managed to elude them. He then sighted two 190s off to his right and attacked, rolling down in a spiral with one of them, firing all the way. The second Focke Wulf used this opportunity to get on Crenshaw's tail. This aircraft was

A P-51D of 353rd Fighter Group banks in a climbing turn

101

sighted by Whisner and he closed on it giving it a deflection shot and then pulled through until he was slightly above the 190. Although he scored strikes all over the cockpit and engine, Whisner had to settle for another probable on this one as his gun camera had run out of film.

Crenshaw, intent on his fifth victim, stuck with his 190 until it stopped rolling at 9,000 feet, got in a good burst and watched it crash near an airfield.

In this particular battle two new inovations that were being utilised by the Mustang pilots were sized up by Crenshaw in his combat report. 'The success of my encounter is attributable to the presence of the Germans as well as the superlative working of my K-14 gunsight and G-suit. The G-suit enabled me to make all the violent maneuvers necessary to protect myself and still be an effective fighting force. The sight allowed me to fire short bursts with astonishing accuracy. I missed on only two bursts, one while firing at 90 degrees deflection and the other while rolling with the enemy aircraft.'

The K-14 sight contained both a fixed and gyro-actuated optical system and computed the correct lead angle for targets at ranges of from 200 to 800 yards. The optical system projected a cross on a reflector glass while the gyro system projected a variable diameter circle of six diamond-shaped pips surrounding a central dot.

The sight was adjusted for the size of the target by means of a span scale. After that, the range was set into the computing mechanism by rotating the throttle grip until the diameter of the gyro image coincided with the span of the target. This was a tremendous advantage over the pure optic head sight with which the pilot had to lay out his own deflection during his attack on an enemy aircraft.

One of the last types of German aircraft to be encountered in Europe was the jet-powered Arado 234 reconnaissance bomber. This craft was initially used late in 1944 to fly missions over

Britian, but during the Battle of the Bulge in December of 1944 it was used over the Continent in both a recce and a bombing role.

One of the first jets to fall to the guns of a Mustang was downed by Lieutenant-Colonel John C Meyer of the 352nd Fighter Group on the last day of 1944. Over Viviers he and his formation spotted one of the new jet craft flying towards the north-east. The squadron turned and the attack was initiated by Captain Bryan who got some hits on the starboard engine of the Arado.

At that moment Colonel Meyer sighted another jet pulling in underneath Captain Bryan. Calling for him to break, Meyer chased the Arado into the overcast. 'I seemed to be neither gaining or losing ground pulling sixty-seven inches of manifold pressure and 3,000rpm,' Meyer related.

'Just west of Bonn the jet went back into the clouds at 10,000 feet and I went under also, losing sight of him. I continued this heading and again sighted

The turbo-jet powered Arado 234 reconnaissance aircraft. This type proved too slow for the P-51 and numbers were destroyed

the craft in a port turn at 5,000 feet above 10/10 cloud cover, with tops at 3,000-4,000 feet. I was able to close and fired two 2-second bursts at 700 and 600 yards, 30 degrees deflection. I saw no strikes but the enemy aircraft jettisoned either his canopy or escape hatch.

'To avoid going into cloud in a vertical bank I broke off the attack and momentarily lost sight of the aircraft. A few seconds later, swinging around small cumulus top of cloud, I saw the craft headed straight down and go into the overcast at 3,000 feet'.

As the Allied forces dashed for the Rhine following the breakthrough into Germany in 1945, more of the Arados put in their appearance. Quite a number were sighted and downed in their attempts to bomb the bridges across the river. However, this jet did not possess the superior speed of the Messerschmitt 262 and could be easily attacked by a diving Mustang.

In December 1944, the 78th Fighter Group became the last fighter unit of the Eighth Air Force to convert to the P-51 Mustang. This gave the organisation fourteen Mustang groups, and only one, the 56th Fighter Group, kept the P-47. The 56th continued to fly their beloved 'Jugs' up until the end of the war.

In early 1945, the RAF began to get some P-51Os, or Mustang Mark IVs as they were known. These new aircraft were utilised primarily as bomber escort for RAF Bomber Command. In view of the air superiority enjoyed by the Allies in 1945 the Lancasters and Halifaxes began to fly daylight missions against German targets rather than restrict their operations to night bombing.

Many of the fighter squadrons of the RAF continued to fly their Mustang Mark IIIs right up to the end of the war. One of the wings that did so was

103

No 133, two of whose squadrons were composed of Polish pilots.

On the afternoon of 9th April 1945, these units took off to escort a heavy bomber attack on Hamburg. That day four of the vaunted Messerschmitt Me 262s fell to the Polish pilots. One of those who scored was Flight Lieutenant M Gorzula.

Gorzula had just come off the target area when six enemy aircraft were sighted some 2,000 yards or more away diving down on the bombers. As he closed on the aircraft they were immediately identified as jet Me 262s. Gorzula dived on the tail of one of the jets at about 500 miles an hour, but the German pilot sighted him and tried to get away. With his superior speed the German began to pull away making it difficult for Gorzula to close under little less than 1,000 yards. However, Gorzula hit his war emergency boost, closed a little and gave the enemy aircraft a squirt from his guns. A second later another burst caused the jet to slow and then Gorzula moved in for the 'kill'. A third burst brought about a flash of fire and the Messerschmitt began to break up. The engines fell away from the fuselage and the enemy craft went down spinning. The pilot bailed out, but he pulled his ripcord too soon. The flaming debris from his craft set fire to the canopy.

The lack of fuel and shortage of pilots had grounded many Luftwaffe aircraft by 1945 and the long-ranging fighter sweeps of the Mustangs took a tremendous toll. It was not unusual for a group to destroy fifty or more enemy aircraft on one strafing mission.

As the retreating Germans tried desperately to pull their forces into Germany for regrouping early in 1945 the Allied aircraft cut deeply into their remaining rail rolling stock and transport. In a brilliant operation in February the Mustangs of the 55th Fighter Group took off in extremely bad weather to go after German rolling stock. The P-51s arrived over the target and flew their strafing mission in the face of very heavy flak. In addi-

tion to wiping out an entire enemy troop train they destroyed 81 locomotives, 53 oil cars, 32 half tracks and 70 armored vehicles.

The following day the 55th went in on the deck once again and braved the flak to hit the German rail system. Once more success was theirs as they broke the record of the previous day by destroying eighty-nine locomotives. Further damage and destruction was wrought on large numbers of goods wagons, oil cars, trucks and also on a power plant and a warehouse. They even set fire to five lumber yards. Four

Mustangs were lost in the two-day operation. With such devastating success, there was little doubt that the German army's ability to move and regroup was seriously crippled.

On 18th March 1945, Major Pierce McKennon of the 4th Fighter Group was involved in one of the more unusual Mustang incidents of the Second World War. While leading his 335th Fighter Squadron in a strafing mission against Prrezlau Airdrome some forty miles from Berlin, his P-51 took a flak hit in the engine. Immediately, he lost oil pressure and realised that

The Luftwaffe burns on the ground. The P-51 from which this was taken is credited with accounting for six of the blazing planes

he would have to bail out.

McKennon maneuvered his aircraft away from a populated area and got ready to go over the side. Halfway out of the aircraft he found himself caught on something in the cockpit. Desperately he tugged and finally tore himself loose and went down, barely missing the tail of the Mustang. He then pulled the ripcord and the chute

Adolf Galland

blossomed over him.

As he got out of his parachute harness he noted a Mustang trying to land in the same meadow in which he had landed. On the third attempt the pilot made it and began to make frantic motions for McKennon to join him. As McKennon ran towards the aircraft he recognised his wingman, George Green. Green got out of the cockpit and McKennon climbed in and dropped the wing tanks to lighten the load. Green got in the cockpit in McKennon's lap.

By this time German soldiers began to run across the meadow towards the Mustang. This threat was thwarted by P-51s from overhead that dove down and made strafing passes causing them to run for cover. Green pushed the throttle all the way forward and the Mustang went rolling down the meadow. Just when it seemed that the craft would crash into a row of trees at the edge of the meadow the Mustang leaped into the air and barely cleared them. Heavy rain and poor visibility forced them to have to climb to 15,000 feet as they flew over Holland and the two pilots had to take turns with the one oxygen mask to keep from blacking out. Two and a half hours later the Mustang came to rest at Debden with two pilots aboard: rescue mission successful.

The most elite enemy organisation that the Mustang ever faced during the Second World War was probably *Jagdverband* 44 flying the Messerschmitt Me 262. This unit was formed under the leadership of General Adolf Galland, who had been dethroned as head of the Luftwaffe Fighter Command in January 1945. Among its complement were ten holders of the coveted German Knight's Cross. JV 44s primary task was the interception and destruction of Allied bombers. They were to tangle with fighters only of necessity.

At about 1100 hours on 26th April 1945, General Galland took off from Munchen/Rien airfield with five other Me 262s to intercept a formation of American bombers. One had to return to base with engine trouble, but the remaining five continued to attack the formation of Martin B-26 Marauders flying in two tight vics of about thirty aircraft each. Coming in at twelve o'clock the German fighters passed over the formation below. Galland, with his wingman, had picked the outside rear flying B-26 of the first vic as his target. As they closed in the B-26 formation recognised them and opened fire before the Messerschmitts did. Galland pulled up and fired his cannon. The Marauder exploded in mid-air. Meanwhile Galland, bypassing the exploding aircraft, lined up on the second but since he failed to release the safety button for his rockets, they did not fire and he only obtained a few cannon hits on his second target.

While banking away to observe the results of his attack on the second B-26, Galland sustained hits in his fuel tanks from the bomber. At the same moment he was attacked by a Mustang. His Me 262 was hit several times in the cockpit and in the engine. Galland sustained splinters in his right leg. Immediately, he dove down to escape his attacker. He was not pursued so he followed the autobahn to his home base to find that it was under attack by P-51s. Due to the fact that he was badly hit, Galland had to take a chance, cut his fuel and come in on a glide approach. Luckily he was able to land without coming under further attack. Four of the Marauders fell to the guns of the Me 262s, nevertheless even such an elite organisation could not operate for long under such odds and their losses in the air and on the ground forced the end of Me 262 operations shortly afterwards.

Allied airpower ruled supreme and the P-51 Mustang had done much to make it possible. The gaudy painted fighters dominated the skies over Germany until the very last. On 8th May 1945, the war in Europe came to an end.

Mustangs from the south

When the US Fifteenth Air Force was activated in Italy in November 1943 as the strategic bombing force in the Mediterranean theater of operations it possessed only three P-38 fighter groups to provide escort. In December the 325th Fighter Group was assigned with P-47s. These four groups did an excellent job when the bomber force was small, but as new units began to arrive it became obvious that more fighter escort units were going to be needed.

The 31st Fighter Group gave up its Spitfires on 2nd April, 1944 and became the first P-51 Mustang unit of the Fifteenth Air Force. While its pilots had come to love the versatile little Spitfire, they were just as exuberant over the performance of the Mustang. They particularly enjoyed the fact that they were able to go far into enemy territory with the bombers and join in aerial combat once more. Late 1943 and early 1944 had seen them operating as a tactical ground support unit for the Allied armies that were

moving up the boot of Italy and there had been few days on which German aircraft had been seen since the Allies had gained air superiority over the front lines.

The 31st flew their first escort mission on 16th April 1944, when they took the B-17s and B-24s to bomb Turnul Severin in Rumania. Before the end of the month the group had won its first Presidential Unit Citation in the Mustang.

On the morning of 21st April the Group took off to escort the bombers to the Ploiești oil refineries. The weather was poor and instructions were radioed from Fifteenth Air Force Headquarters that the mission was to be aborted. However, Major James G Thorsen, leading the 31st, failed to get the order.

Thorsen performed an excellent job

14th Air Force P-51D over Italy. The onset of the Italian based Allied bombing offensive demanded more fighter protection

of navigation and found the unescorted bombers in the vicinity of Bucharest preparing for their bomb run over Ploiesti, some sixty miles away. Almost at the point of rendezvous some sixty enemy fighters were sighted several thousand feet above, heading for the bombers.

The Mustangs of the 31st gave combat at once. In a wild and wooly air battle the P-51s downed seventeen enemy aircraft for the loss of only two of their own. One of the leaders that day was Captain John M Ainley who blasted three of the German fighters and claimed another probable. The bombers completed their mission unmolested.

Early in May 1944 the 52nd Fighter Group gave up its Spitfires and became the second Mustang unit in the Fifteenth Air Force. Later that month the veteran 325th Fighter Group traded in its P-47 Thunderbolts for Mustangs.

The success of both units was immediate. The 325th Group 'Checkertails' were elected to escort the first Russian shuttle mission from Italy. Sixty-four P-51s got off on the morning of 2nd June 1944, and escorted the bombers which hit a rail centre at Debrecen, Hungary, and continued on to Russian bases. The mission encountered no enemy fighter opposition and the Russian bases were found without difficulty.

The American fliers met with a most enthusiastic reception from the Russians and songs were sung and toasts of fiery vodka were drunk far into the night. Souvenirs were exchanged and that night a dance was held for the Mustang pilots with Russian girls who served as waitresses in the mess providing dancing partners.

On 6th June the Mustangs escorted a bombing mission that had been planned by the Russian commanders. The Fortresses hit targets at Galati, Rumania and on this mission the Luftwaffe put in an appearance.

Leading his flight after a Junkers Ju 88 that was heading for the bombers, Lieutenant Cullen J Hoffman became the first American pilot to shoot down an enemy plane while flying from Russian bases. 'I fired from dead astern,' he reported, 'and my burst walked up his fuselage and out the right wing until they struck the engine. The plane caught fire and exploded'. Other victories were scored by the Group Commander, Colonel Sluder, and Lieutenant Wayne Lowry, who was to become a high scoring Fifteenth Air Force ace, got his first victory by downing a Focke Wulf 190.

The 52nd Fighter Group was not long in stealing the limelight. On 9th June they were assigned the task of escorting the heavy bombers to Munich. In the course of the mission the bombers became badly scattered and the Luftwaffe sought to take advantage of the situation. Large formations of German fighters came up to challenge the bombers and the 52nd had to disperse its fighters by flights to provide the maximum of protection over a wide area. Through the determination of the Mustang pilots the German fighters were broken up and the bombers were able to drop their bombs successfully. Thirteen of the German fighters fell before the onrushing Mustangs of the 52nd Group. None of the P-51s were lost.

A second Russian shuttle mission was flown on 22nd July 1944, with the Mustangs of the 31st Fighter Group flying top cover for the P-38s of the 82nd Fighter Group. The Lightnings were to strafe the oil refineries at Ploiesti, Rumania, while the P-51s flew top cover for them.

Once the task force had crossed the River Danube the planes let down through the clouds and more than seventy P-38s and fifty Mustangs swept across in strafing runs on Buzău and Zilistea airdromes and their sattelite strips. Devastation was the descriptive word of the day. Some forty-one German planes were left burning or destroyed on the ground. In addition, the task force knocked out six locomotives, three trucks and

Above: 'Checkertails' of 325th Group warming up at a base in Russia. *Below:* The first 8th Air Force Bombardment Group to arrive at a Soviet base is welcomed by Russian military

numerous railway carriages.

One Heinkel III was caught on take off and shot down, and aerial battles then developed that saw fourteen more enemy aircraft being shot down. The task force then proceeded to their Soviet bases.

Three days later, on 25th July, the Lightnings and Mustangs took off from Russia to strafe Mielec Aerodrome which was located 120 miles west of L'vov, Poland. Aircraft from this base were supporting German ground forces in the area. The strafing attack by the P-38s was successful and the aerial battle which took place on the way home was a greater victory. The P-51s of the 31st Group sighted a mixed formation of thirty-six Junkers Ju 87 Stuka dive bombers, four Junkers Ju 52 transports and one reconnaissance 'Storch' flying at low altitude en route to attack Russian ground forces.

The battle took place in an area estimated to cover no more than two square miles, located just behind the Russian lines. The enemy planes were taken by surprise in the diving attack and there was a mass melee as the Stuka pilots attempted to salvo their bombs and get away from the Mustangs. The entire battle took some thirty minutes and when it was over the 31st Group had taken a toll of twenty-seven enemy aircraft destroyed, three probably destroyed and six damaged for a total of thirty-six claims. There were no losses.

The following day the Mustangs took leave of their Russian bases and flew back to San Savero in Italy. On the way the P-51s and Lightnings dropped down to ground level once more and strafed airfields and targets of opportunity in the Bucharest-Ploiesti area. A number of enemy aircraft were destroyed on the ground and several more locomotives were put out of commission. In the Bucharest area German fighters rose to challenge and several of them fell victim to the Mustangs.

In what was perhaps their most

Above left: More B-17s land in Russia after attacking targets in German occupied Europe. *Above:* Shuttle mission to Russia by P-51-escorted Fortresses. *Below:* Soviet airmen and US pilot relax between operations on a Russian airfield

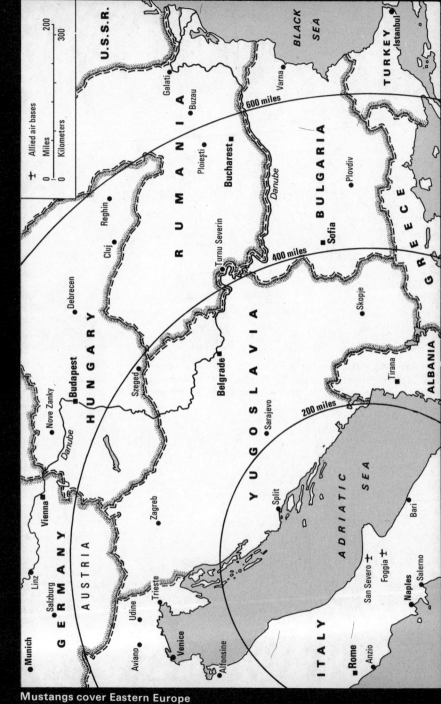

Mustangs cover Eastern Europe

brilliant performance of the war the 31st Fighter Group returned from the shuttle mission with thirty-seven enemy aircraft destroyed in the air. The most impressive achievement, however, was the fact that not one single P-51 was lost on the entire mission: a real tribute to the pilots and the magnificent ground crews that supported them.

In June 1944 the 332nd all-Negro Fighter Group was equipped with Mustangs and they began to take their toll on escort missions during July. On such a mission Captain Joseph D Elsberry used his skill and the maneuverability of his Mustang to bring down three enemy aircraft.

Flying in bad weather the P-51s of the 332nd became scattered, but the rendezvous was still made two minutes early and still the fighters had to wait five minutes for the arrival of the bombers. Just as the coast of southern France was crossed Elsberry sighted a group of enemy fighters beginning to break down in trail to attack the end of the bomber formation. Immediately, the Mustangs dropped their tanks and pulled in on the rear of the enemy formation.

Elsberry fired one burst at a Focke Wulf 190 at long range but saw no result. Then one of the 190s turned right in front of him. The Mustang pilot slammed the throttles forward to pull right in on the rear of the 190. A long burst caused an explosion on the fuselage of the German aircraft and it went down in flames. As the first fighter was going down Elsberry sighted another Focke Wulf turning across his nose. Reefing the Mustang in tightly, he fired while in the turn. The 190 burst into flames and went down. Then a third 190 shot across Elsberry's Mustang. Immediately he went into the turn with it, but the German splitessed and dived for the deck. Elsberry scored good hits on the Focke Wulf before he broke off the attack at approximately 11,000 feet. As Elsberry pulled up he continued to follow the progress of the German

plane. Apparently the pilot thought that he still had the Mustang on his tail for he continued to dive. At the last moment he attempted to pull out, but it was too late. The Focke Wulf flew into the ground.

By August 1944 aerial opposition in the Mediterranean theater had begun to fall off sharply. As the Russian army began to push into the Balkans the Mustangs of the Fifteenth Air Force went down to the deck to hit the Luftwaffe planes that were hampering the advance.

Photo reconnaissance aircraft had pinpointed some 175 single- and twin-engined fighters, dive bombers and transport aircraft on the aerodrome at Reghin in Rumania. The task of eliminating this thorn in the side of Allied operations was assigned to the pilots of the 52nd Fighter Group.

On 31st August the Mustangs of the 52nd flew through bad weather to get to the target. With one squadron flying top cover, two squadrons of the P-51s struck the landing grounds. Estimates placed the number of enemy aircraft destroyed at over a hundred. Attacking from every angle, the Mustang pilots flew from three to six strafing passes each and hit every plane on the ground. When the attack was broken off the field was a mass of flaming and broken aircraft. To complete the day's achievements, the top cover squadron downed nine enemy aircraft over the aerodrome.

Boedecker reported that 'The field was a furnace of burning planes with the smoke and flames rising high into the air. I've never before seen a place get such a pasting as we gave that aerodrome'.

On 10th September the 325th Fighter Group flew a similar mission that was quite successful. Colonel Chester L Sluder led the Mustangs against the aerodrome at Ecka, Yugoslavia and left all of the forty enemy aircraft on the field destroyed. Five to eight passes were flown by each pilot and only one Mustang was lost to flak.

'There wasn't much ground fire at

Lieutenant-General Eaker, C-in-C
Mediterranean Allied Air Forces, talks
to a US pilot in Russia

all,' said Lieutenant Robert H Brown,
'and that made it a lot of fun. One
machine gun nest at the end of the
field was taken care of in a hurry'.

Lieutenant David Schmebeck said,
'There was so much smoke rising from
the field when we left that the place
looked like one of the old bombing
attacks on the Ploiesti oil fields'.

The Mustangs of the AAF were not
the only ones taking toll of enemy
installations in the Mediterranean:
the Mustang IIIs of No 112 Squadron,
RAF, were also hitting ground targets
in the theater. Twelve Mustangs under
the leadership of Group Captain Eaton,
DSO, were airborne on the morning
of 6th September 1944, to fly an armed
reconnaissance mission in the Udine
area of Italy.

Initial attacks were flown against a
5,000-ton motor vessel and a number of
smaller tugs. However, the bombs fell
short. Four airfields were then recon-
noitred with better results. The last
airfield housed seven Junkers Ju 87s
and one Focke Wulf 190 which were
strafed. All the aircraft were hit and
the 190 was smoking when the Mustangs departed.

The aircraft took leave of the scene
of destruction and went after locomotives. One train pulling seven carriages was sighted and the Mustangs
swooped down with guns blazing. The
engineer immediately left the cab and
the fighters worked the train over
until they were out of ammunition.
Then the Mustangs headed for home.

Three days later a pilot of No 112
Squadron spotted a 2,000-ton, one-
funnel ship. The Mustangs bombed it
and Sergeant Williams put a 1,000-
lb bomb right in the funnel area. The
ship made for shore listing heavily
and beached itself.

After attacking some barges the
Mustangs flew on to Crado and found a
train. The engine was destroyed and
the fighter planes continued to Rivol-

to airfield where they strafed four enemy fighter planes. The next target was another train whose locomotive was quickly put out of commission.

Aviano airfield furnished the Mustangs targets in the form of six Savoia Marchetti SM 79 aircraft, all of which were strafed and damaged. The Mustangs then headed for home but the day was not yet over. Another locomotive and a Heinkel He III parked on a small airfield were destroyed on the way.

On one of the 31st Group's strafing missions Lieutenant Charles E Wilson became the victim of his own target. As Wilson swooped down on a locomotive that was pulling into a station with its string of box cars a burst from his guns into the engine sent up steel fragments that damaged his aircraft so badly that he was forced to make a belly landing some five miles outside the town.

Major Wyatt P Exum put his P-51 down in the ditch-encircled field to pick him up. Wilson got into the cockpit with Exum and they managed to get the Mustang back into the air, though they had to hop one ditch to get airborne.

Exum recorded that the one disconcerting thing about the flight back was the fact that 'Wilson's feet were pressed against the instrument panel and he kept kicking off the ignition. I didn't like that, but all in all it was a pretty cooperative job – Wilson read all the instruments I couldn't see. He knew the way home and I didn't'.

In November 1944, No 3 Squadron, Royal Australian Air Force, was equipped with Mustangs which they quickly put to good use. The range of the new aircraft enabled them to go far into the Balkans to carry out bombing and strafing attacks where

A causeway at Mantua is cut in a mission to disrupt enemy supply lines

they had been pretty well restricted to front line support over Italy with their Curtiss Kittyhawks.

The pilots of No 3 Squadron were also very impressed with the ability of the Mustang to take punishment and still come home. On one mission a pilot returned 265 miles to base with no rudder control. Half of the elevator had been shot off and the rear section of the fuselage was damaged by fire.

Normally the Mustangs of No 3 Squadron carried either 500- or 1,000-lb bombs, but in January 1945 they helped pioneer another type of mission. The aircraft were loaded with 750-lb napalm bombs. On the morning of 2nd January, twelve Mustangs set out to attack an enemy troop position in the vicinity of Alfonsine. Six Mustangs initiated the attack by dropping 500-lb high explosive bombs. They were followed by the other six aircraft of the squadron with their napalm. Once their incendiary explosives hit the ground destruction was complete as flames a hundred feet high shot into the air.

Although the Luftwaffe was not often encountered in spring 1945, there were occasions when they did battle in the air and then the action was fast and furious. The 325th Fighter Group was returning from an escort mission to Nove Zanky, Hungary on 14th March 1945, when three of its Mustang pilots sighted two Me 109s attacking a Russian bomber formation. They pursued the Messerschmitts from 25,000 to 16,000 feet, destroying one of them and sending the other off smoking.

A few moments later one of the 'Checkertail' Mustangs let down through the overcast due to an oxygen shortage. As the pilot broke out he found himself gazing on a large gaggle of thirty-four Focke Wulf 190s. He called his squadron mates on the radio and then attacked the closest 190. Eleven more Mustangs dropped down through the low clouds and a massive dogfight took place. When the din of battle had subsided, seventeen of the Focke Wulf 190s had been destroyed for

the loss of two Mustangs. One of the lost Mustang pilots had crash-landed behind the Russian lines and was back in Italy within a few days.

In 1945 operations for the Mustang pilots of the Fifteenth Air Force reached their zenith on 24th March. That day all four Mustang units were briefed to escort the bombers on a 1,500-mile round trip to Berlin. The pilots of the Mediterranean had never seriously believed they would ever see the capitol city of the Third Reich and the briefing was received with much enthusiasm.

Most of the pilots on that mission saw nothing of enemy aircraft. They

had to be content with the sight of the B-17s' bombs falling on the Daimler Benz Tank Works. However, for other pilots there was great excitement. Some twenty-five Messerschmitt Me 262 jets came up to oppose the bombers on the way home. Five of the Me 262s were downed by the 308th Squadron of the 31st Fighter Group. Colonel William Daniel, Group CO, got the first when he dived on the tail-end Charlie of a jet formation. A long range burst sent the craft into a snap roll and then caused the plane to explode.

Lieutenant William M Wilder got into position just as one of the jets was

A moment of drama as a returning B-17 lands with port outboard engine afire

lining up on the bombers. 'I hit the right engine and a lot of smoke began to come out. The German bailed out'. Captain Kenneth T Smith's victim also bailed out as he was firing at it. Lieutenant Ray D Leonard got the fourth jet as it attempted to make a pass at one of the bombers: 'My shots started it smoking and it pulled up in a slight climb to the left. I kept shooting and the pieces flew off. Both engines caught fire and the pilot bailed out.

The 332nd Fighter Group also en-

countered some of the Me 262s and its pilots downed three of them. Lieutenant Roscoe C Brown got one of the jets on his tail, feinted to one side and then broke to the other, causing the jet to overshoot him. He than latched onto the tail of the Me 262 and shot it down.

A most unusual combat took place on the afternoon of 31st March, when a formation of P-51s encountered four Focke Wulf 190s practising gunnery on ground targets. The four Mustangs attacked and shot three of them down out of their pattern. The fourth flew off into the haze and escaped.

In one of the last major air battles in the Mediterranean the 332nd Fighter Group chanced upon several flights of enemy aircraft in the Linz-Salzburg area. Thirteen German fighters were shot from the sky in the ensuing dogfights. Lieutenant Robert Williams got one Focke Wulf 190 while he was trying to get away from another German fighter on his tail. The enemy aircraft turned across his nose as he was taking a turn in evasive action. Williams gave him a long burst and the Focke Wulf went into a steep dive and crashed.

Major Robert F Johnson of the 325th Fighter Group got the last German jet to fall to the Fifteenth Air Force fighters on 18th April 1945. Johnson sighted the jet as it began to take off from its aerodrome near Munich, Germany. Diving down from 10,000 feet he hit it as it was only about ten feet off the ground. The jet went into a climbing turn to the left and Johnson kept firing until at approximately 3,000 feet the enemy aircraft rolled over and the pilot bailed out.

The Mustangs of the Mediterranean had been triumphant not only in the air but destroyed vast quantities of enemy vehicles on the ground and crippled his railroads as they went along. The P-51 had made just as impressive a record in the southern theater as it had flying from England.

Against the
rising sun

The Mustang arrived in the China-Burma-India theater of operations as property of the 311th Fighter Group. Their first assignment was the defense of the Brahmaputra Valley, protection of the northern air route to China and offensive operations in Northern Burma in preparation for a drive to the south by General Stilwell's Chinese-American ground forces. The aircraft would be operating over three countries from the very beginning.

This called for initial dispersal of the three squadrons of the 311th. All moved to bases in northern Assam; one squadron of A-36s went to Sookerating, one squadron of P-51As went to Dinjan and the third squadron, also flying P-51As, was sent to Mohanbari. Their first mission took place on 16th October 1943, when eight A-36s bombed and strafed the town of Sumprebum in northern Burma.

From that day on, the A-36s and P-51s of the 311th continued to attack various towns and villages occupied by the Japanese. An effective ground Intelligence system made it possible for the pilots of the 311th to make life miserable for the enemy during those early months of operations.

Late in November of 1943 the 530th Fighter Squadron of the 311th Group was sent down to Kurmitola, India, to provide escort for B-24s of the 7th Bomb Group and B-25s of the 490th Bomb Group that were carrying out their bombing operations in the Rangoon area. This long range escort called for the P-51s to cover a distance of some 650 miles one way against very strong enemy fighter opposition.

One of the young American pilots flying these missions was Lieutenant J J England. 'I flew three of these escort missions', England related, 'on one mission I had only five P-51s to escort a squadron of B-24s at maximum range for the Mustangs. The so-called Japanese 'Black Dragons' were

'Candy-stripe' P-51s over the Chin Hills, Burma

B-24s escorted by P-51s and P-40s en route to raid a Japanese supply point

operating in the Rangoon area at that time and they were all very good pilots. They gave us hell. We lost eight pilots on the three missions including our Group Commander. We were never able to determine whether all were lost to enemy fire or to lack of fuel. I had a wingman shot off my wing on the first mission. The roughest part of these missions was not being able to operate at full throttle. We had to limit our fight to 20 minutes and get back under the B-24s.'

The intensity of these brief operations is indicated by the fact that the Mustangs downed seventeen Japanese aircraft in their encounters.

The 311th Fighter Group continued to fly strikes against Japanese installations and lines of communication during late 1943 and early 1944. Often the Mustangs were utilized as top cover for troop carrier squadrons dropping food and supplies to the Chinese divisions that were driving south down the Hukawng Valley. Constant bombing and strafing of the Japanese airfields at Myitkyina and Bhamo prevented the enemy from harassing the Chinese from the air.

Flight-Officer Hoyt M Hensley and Lieutenant Cecil Blow were flying one of the support missions for C-47s on 18th January, 1944, when enemy fighters were encountered. The two P-51s sighted at least four enemy aircraft in combat with four P-51s at 4,000 feet and two miles away at the nine o'clock position. At the same time another flight of four enemy fighters was sighted one mile away in the eleven o'clock position at 10,000 feet. The three escorted C-47s were two miles behind Hensley and Blow at a very low altitude heading south-east. At that time the top four enemy aircraft peeled off into a dive and headed towards the fight taking place at 4,000 feet. Hensley and Blow apparently had not been sighted and they dived to the attack.

Lieutenant Blow made two passes on two different Hamps with unobserved results. On his third pass he came in from a ten o'clock position and above the Hamp. Good strikes were registered on the top of the fuselage and wings but no smoke or fire emerged. The Hamp splitessed and dived for the deck. By this time the enemy formation had split and started a run for home.

Hensley followed Blow down in the dive and fired a short burst at a Zeke with unobserved results. Pulling out on the deck he climbed back to 7,000 feet and sighted another Zeke 2,000 feet below him. Hensley dived once more and caught the Zeke as it attempted to turn into his attack. The enemy aircraft took the full force of a burst in the cockpit area and slipped off into a dive from which it did not recover.

The two Mustang pilots joined up and returned to base. The C-47s were unmolested in their mission.

On 8th March, 1944, the Mustangs of the 311th Group began flying air support for 'Merrill's Marauders', an American infantry unit, which was spearheading the attack by the Chinese in their attempt to take the entire Hukawng Valley. An American Air Force officer had been assigned to each battalion to direct the bombing and strafing by the planes by use of ground to air radio. This system was so successful that by the end of the month the Mustangs were dropping bombs within fifty yards of the forward troops.

Lieutenant William L Fleming was one of the air liaison officers who was assigned to the Marauders. At one time his unit was surrounded by the Japanese who brought heavy artillery fire to bear upon it. Captain Roland J

A Mustang raises a little dust taking off from road air base in India

A captured Japanese 'Hamp', suitably dressed with USAAF markings, is studied in flight to evaluate its performance

Migues' squadron of A-36s was assigned the air support of this unit.

Often Fleming directed the fighters against artillery positions within 200 yards of the American positions. For twenty-six days the fighter-bombers swept over the Japanese positions hourly, strafing and bombing with amazing accuracy. When this failed to dislodge the enemy, the pilots doubled their missions and attacked every thirty minutes. After a week of this hammering the Japanese guns were silenced. The Marauders then continued their advance which culminated in the capture of Myitkyina airfield.

On 27th March the Japanese made their last large full scale attempt to knock out the bases of the 311th Group in the Brahmaputra Valley. Some fifteen Japanese bombers escorted by some thirty fighters were reported heading for the American installations and the Mustangs were scrambled. Interception was made before the bases could be reached and in the ensuing air battle four of the enemy aircraft were downed, their formations broken up and the attack thwarted.

During May 1944 one squadron of the 311th under the command of Major S M Newcombe was called south to be based at Dohazari, India (now East Pakistan). It was the mission of this unit to assist in knocking out the Japanese Air Force's attempt to give air support to their beleaguered troops in the Myitkyina and Imphal areas. During a four-day period, the squadron shot down twenty-four enemy aircraft without a single loss to themselves.

In the course of one of the air battles the Mustangs were credited with knocking thirteen of twenty-five Japanese fighters out of the sky, with several more probably destroyed and damaged. Major Newcombe described

the actions as follows: 'We reached the Irrawaddy River and went on to Meiktila airfield. We gradually reduced altitude to 16,000 feet. No Japanese planes were visible, so we went on to Aungbun, where I saw two enemy planes in the air. I delegated a section to drop its long range tanks and attack, but quickly realized the Japanese were there in force.

'There were about 29 of them. They were all flying close together. The whole squadron then went in to attack them. I noticed the enemy were of pretty poor caliber and showed a tendancy to fly in formations of two and four, presumably for protection. I dived out of the sun onto the tail of two of them and gave one of them a short burst at 20 yards.

'The enemy plane seemed to belch flame out of its engine and cockpit

Rocket firing P-51s begin to be used in Burma in the summer of 1944

and explosions shook its wing roots. It seemed to me the skill of the Japanese pilots was very poor. Not one of my boys got a scratch.'

During summer 1944 the 311th Fighter Group began to use rockets on their P-51Bs in direct support of the British who were working back south along the railroad corridor from Moguang. Fighter sweeps were flown over the Japanese fields in Central Burma forcing the enemy to use these fields for staging areas only. By this time air supremacy by the Americans was such that little enemy opposition was encountered.

The 23rd Fighter Group in China had been receiving a smattering of Mustangs from late 1943, but it was summer 1944 before they really had enough P-51s to put them to good use. Of particular import was the magnificent work they did against enemy targets during June 1944.

An example of the excellent work of the 23rd Group Mustangs would be their operations of 18th June. On that morning Captain John C 'Pappy' Herbst took off in his P-51 to make a weather reconnaissance in the Ch'angsha area. He found the weather fine and in the course of his mission Herbst found time to go down and strafe several group of cavalry, killing some fifteen Japanese troops.

On his return, twelve P-51s took off to dive bomb and strafe the Ch'angsha area. Upon arrival, a 200-foot gunboat was spotted, bombed and sunk. A 50-foot boat was razed and six barges were damaged. There was no enemy air opposition so the Mustangs returned to base for fuel and ammunition.

After servicing, fourteen Mustangs took off to attack shipping on the Siang Chiang River. Finding a group of thirteen small barges, the Mustangs broke into trail formation and took turns strafing until all had been destroyed. After lunch the Mustangs were loaded with bombs and refueled and dispatched to hit targets of opportunity in the area of Shayunkang.

While on a bomb run twelve Oscar fighters came down to oppose the P-51s. Three of the Oscars fell to the guns of the American pilots who emerged unscathed. During the air battle one Mustang chose to go down to the deck and shoot up ten trucks on the ground.

To finish the day, ten Mustangs bombed the town of Tanganchow. Compounds, houses and six camouflaged barges were hit in the area. No enemy fighters came up to challenge the Americans, so the Mustang pilots called an end to a very busy day and came home.

The P-51s of the 23rd Group not only did bombing and strafing on their own, but were utilised to a great extent for bomber and fighter escort work. The B-25s of the Fourteenth Air Force depended upon them for top cover on their bombing missions as did the P-40s of the command. The Mustangs quite often operated as they did on the morning of 19th June, 1944, when they escorted the P-40s to Lukow. Once the older fighters were through, the P-51s went to work. After they had bombed Lukow the Mustangs strafed and riddled a pontoon bridge. Then they climbed back to altitude and brought the P-40s home.

In summer 1944, the 118th Tactical Reconnaissance Squadron joined the 23rd Fighter Group. This unit not only proved itself in its primary task but also became a fighting and bombing organisation. By late 1944 they began to excel in skip and dive bombing against shipping. One of their outstanding missions was flown on 8th December when they dispatched thirteen Mustangs to go after shipping in the harbor at Hong Kong.

Four of the P-51s were laden with two 500-lb demolition bombs each and the rest carried one 500-lb bomb each. Captain Meyers, who was leading the skip bomb flight, chose as his target a 500-foot transport in the harbor. Two direct hits were scored on the vessel and as soon as he pulled up Lieutenant Egan made his run and

Above: One of numerous raids on Japanese shipping in the South China Sea
Below: P-40; now overtaken in performance, P-40s have P-51 escort on their missions

put two more bombs into the ship. The transport burst into flames and was observed sinking at the stern.

The balance of the P-51 pilots succeeded in putting bombs into a 500-foot freighter and a 250-foot freighter which were left burning. Three other freighters were damaged.

The flight re-formed off the southeast end of Hong Kong Island and proceeded to fly a fighter sweep against Tok Pak Uk airdrome. Several passes were made on a Topsy type transport until it finally exploded. A Tojo type fighter attempted to take off but it was destroyed before it could become airborne. All the Mustangs returned safely.

In a classic two-aircraft mission, Lieutenant-Colonel Ed McComas and his wingman, Lieutenant Parnell, used the element of surprise to get three direct hits on a Japanese des-

Mustangs of 118th Tactical Reconnaissance Squadron on their base in China

troyer. The two Mustangs proceeded to a point approximately forty miles north-east of Hong Kong harbor and then came in for a high speed run just skimming the water. Before the Japanese were aware that they were under attack, McComas had put his bomb amidships of the destroyer. Parnell came in right behind him and dropped two bombs in the same place.

The Mustang pilots never looked back but re-formed on the south side of Hong Kong and headed north to strafe Tak Pak Uk airdrome. Here they picked up heavy anti-aircraft fire, but Parnell still managed to destroy two aircraft on his strafing run before the Mustangs raced for home.

As 1944 drew to a close the Mustangs of the 23rd Group continued to keep Japanese airpower grounded by constantly attacking their airfields. The

Lieutenant-Colonel Ed McComas, a top scoring Mustang ace in China with fourteen victories

133

outstanding feature of these missions was that the Mustangs were able to attack Japanese aircraft after they had already performed another type of mission such as bombing shipping and harbor installations.

McComas led an outstanding mission of this variety on 24th December when he and fifteen other Mustang pilots took off on a skip bombing mission against the Wu-ch'ang ferry terminals. Upon arrival in the target area the formation broke into two bomb flights and one cover flight which would orbit north of the target.

Lieutenant Peterson led his flight against the Wu-ch'ang side where several hits and near misses were scored on the ferry slips. Peterson was to have hit the Wu-ch'ang airdrome after bombing the ferry, but his flight missed it so they proceeded to strafe and set fire to three oil storage tanks.

As Lieutenant Russel D Williams pulled off his bomb run and climbed for altitude he sighted twelve Oscars above and behind him. He turned back into them and finally caught onto the tail of one of them at 6,000 feet. He fired a long burst at the Oscar and observed strikes on the fuselage. As Williams closed to within twenty-five yards of the craft he gave it another burst and watched it burst into flames. The Mustang pilot then went down on the deck to strafe a Japanese bomber on the ground.

Lieutenant Grover pulled up off the target after dropping his bomb and cruised right up on the tail of an Oscar which he immediately shot down. Grover was then jumped by two Oscars. He put the Mustang into a dive, pulled up and came in on the tail of his opponents who had given up trying to catch him going down. Grover opened fire, the Oscar splitessed, but the P-51 pilot hung right with him, firing all the way. The Oscar continued his dive into the ground.

McComas shot up one Japanese bomber and one fighter on the ground in strafing passes when he sighted six

Oscars above him as he pulled up. One Oscar tailed him and scored hits in his wing, but McComas dived away and then climbed to 7,000 feet and tailed an Oscar. A long burst hit the Oscar in the wing root. The pilot jettisoned the canopy and bailed out.

As McComas passed over Tao Kow airfield he observed nine Oscars preparing to take off. He circled and made a west to east pass on two Oscars just as they cleared the runway. A good burst caused one Oscar to flip over and crash into the other and both crashed just east of the field. McComas then pulled in behind two more Oscars as they took off abreast. McComas closed in to fifty yards before he opened fire and put a long burst into each one of them. Both of them crashed to the ground. McComas climbed, assembled his P-51s and returned to base.

P-40s and two P-51s at Karachi

The sixteen Mustangs had heavily damaged the Wu-ch'ang Han-k'ou ferry slips, burned three oil storage tanks, shot down eight Japanese fighters and destroyed five more aircraft on the ground, all in one mission.

Some of the last Mustang air-to-air action in China took place in January 1945 when the P-51s ranged into the Shanghai area to sweep the airfields. On 18th January, Lieutenant-Colonel Charles Older led a flight of eight Mustangs from the 118th Tac Recon Squadron and twelve from the 74th Fighter Squadron on the mission.

Colonel Older led the way by getting on the tail of a Sonia attack bomber when he got in the target area. This he shot down and as he came off his pass he sighted a Betty bomber and a Tess transport aircraft on the deck north-east of Yachang near the river. He came behind each in turn and sent both of them crashing into the river bank.

Older then came back to Tachang where he made four strafing passes on the airfield, destroying three Lily bombers, probably destroying two more and damaging a single engine transport plane.

Repeated passes on the airfield left it covered with burning and wrecked aircraft. Light Japanese ground fire failed to bring down any Mustangs.

Although the P-51s saw extensive action against ground targets until the end of the war, the air-to-air war against the Japanese was all but over by the end of January 1945. The Mustang did yeoman duty in the China-Burma-India theatre where it fulfilled successfully every mission that was asked of it.

135

While the Mustangs were enjoying success in the European theater in 1944, General George C Kenney, Commander of the Fifth Air Force, was doing his best to obtain some P-51s for his command in the South-West Pacific. Despite his persistence, it was late in 1944 before any Mustangs arrived in the theater. Some photo reconnaissance versions – or F-6s as they were designated – and some P-51s were initially assigned to the 82nd Tactical Reconnaissance Squadron then based at San José on the island of Mindoro in the Philippines.

The 82nd had been doing considerable recce work on Japanese movements and airfields. It was on such a mission that Captain William A Shomo won the Congressional Medal of Honor flying a Mustang. He and his wingman, Lieutenant Paul M Lipscomb, took off from their base to check airdromes in northern Luzon to see whether or not the Japanese were using the strips.

While flying at only 200 feet, just south-west of Baguio, they spotted a twin-engined Japanese bomber being escorted by twelve Tony type fighters. The formation was some 2,000 feet above them and had apparently failed to notice them. The Americans realised that for the lone bomber to have such protection it must be occupied by some very important people.

Shomo and Lipscomb climbed steeply to make the interception. As the two Mustang pilots opened fire, the Japanese continued to hold formation and pay no attention to the P-51s. Either the Americans were not spotted until it was too late or the enemy pilots mistook the Mustangs, which were new to the theater, to be two more Tonys coming up to join the formation.

Shomo promptly shot down the bomber while Lipscomb destroyed one of the fighters. This broke up the

More than one hundred Mustangs on Iwo Jima – within reach of the Japanese home islands

Mustangs in
the Pacific

General George C Kenny. He had to wait till late 1944 before his South West Pacific command was allowed P-51s

enemy formation and the Tonys appeared to mill around in confusion. The Mustangs continued to tear into the enemy fighters and nothing the Tony pilots did seemed to be right. When the combat was broken, Shomo had downed six of the enemy fighters in addition to the bomber and Lipscomb had downed four fighters. The two surviving Tonys left at high speed for Formosa.

The Third Air Commando Group's P-51s arrived in the Philippines in early January 1945 and the unit began operations on the 8th of the month. Many of the pilots in this organisation were veterans of the air war over Europe and had quite a number of victories to their credit. However, it was not their fortune to encounter the enemy to any degree in the Philippines. Most of the Japanese aircraft

in the area had been soundly defeated by that time and the Mustang pilots had to be content to fly missions against ground targets. This they did with great success. Bombing, strafing and using rockets, the 3rd Air Commandos destroyed enemy gun emplacements, ammunition dumps, lines of communication and troop concentrations up to the end of the Philippines campaign.

In November 1944, the Boeing B-29s of the Twentieth Bomber Command started their bombing campaign against the Japanese home islands, flying from their new bases on Saipan and Tinian in the Marianas. These early missions encountered little enemy fighter opposition, but the bomber commanders were well aware that as the campaign proceeded and the Japanese pulled in their forces for the last great battle, opposition would increase beyond measure. Long range escort for the bombers would be essential and the plane for the job was the P-51 Mustang.

First, a base had to be established that would be within range of the P-51s. The invasion of this potential base was begun on 19th February, 1945, when the US Marines invaded the island of Iwo Jima. As soon as the beachhead had been established, the Seabee construction batallions arrived to start building the 5,000-foot runways that would accomodate the fighter planes.

On 6th March, 1945, the 15th Fighter Group arrived on the new South Field strip and began its operations at once. They were joined on the 15th of the month by the 21st Fighter Group. These two units flew a number of missions against other ground targets in the island chain as they gained combat proficiency for the very long range escort missions that were to come.

The Mustang pilots did not have long to wait. On the morning of 7th April, 1945, 108 P-51s of the 15th and 21st Fighter Groups were airborne on their way to rendezvous with 107 B-29s of the 73rd Bombardment Wing. The target was the Nakamima Aircraft Plant in Tokyo.

The Mustangs met the bombers at Kozu and took up their positions on both flanks and slightly ahead of the bombers who were flying at 15,000 feet. Approximately forty-five miles from the target the Japanese interception force made its initial appearance. Practically every type of fighter the enemy owned got into the fight with Nicks, Tojos, Irvings, Tonys and Zekes predominating. However, all the Japanese craft did their best to avoid combat with the Mustangs and concentrated on the bombers.

The Mustang of 71st Tactical Reconnaissance Group flown by Major William Shomo on the mission which gained him the Congressional Medal of Honor

Above: 'Tony' inline engine fighter of the Japanese army. *Below:* The natural choice to escort the B-29 Superfortresses is the Mustang

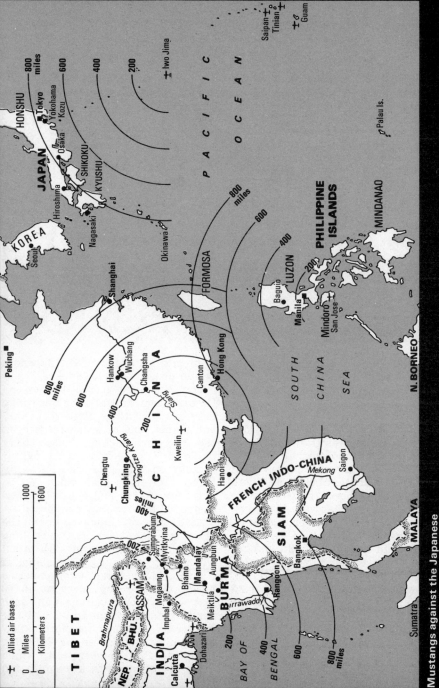

Mustangs against the Japanese

Suffering critical damage inflicted by Japanese AA fire, this P-51 just manages the return trip to newly conquered Iwo Jima

Captain Robert W Moore of the 15th Fighter Group was leading Green Flight on his squadron that day. His unit did not make any passes until they were over the Chosi area where they left the bombers at 22,000 feet to go after four Hamps that were doing lazy eights in loose string over the bombers. Captain Moore joined up as the fifth man in the Hamp flight and got a short burst using twenty-degree deflection at number four Hamp. He saw it explode. Moore then started firing at 600 feet and caught number three Hamp in the formation at the bottom of a lazy eight. Hits were registered in the engine and cockpit. Another burst set the enemy craft on fire, but at that time Moore received a call to break for he was being attacked from the one o'clock position. The Mustang pilot broke immediately and

went into a steep dive. The Japanese fighter chose not to follow.

The Mustangs scored twenty-one times on their initial very long range missions and themselves lost only two planes, one of which ditched on the way home. They successfully broke up the concentrated fighter attacks on the B-29s who lost only three aircraft, two of which fell to anti-aircraft fire and one which was destroyed by air to air bombing.

As a sign of things to come the Mustangs flew their first very long range fighter strike on 16th April when they attacked the island of Kuyshu. At the target two squadrons flew protective top cover at 16,000 feet while two squadrons went into the target area at minimum altitude to strafe. Another squadron flew medium altitude cover for VMF 612, a Marine PBJ bomber unit, which made a rocket attack coordinated

Mustang and Superfortress bound for Japan

A strong defensive formation guards
the 'shepherd' (Boeing B-29) closely

with the fighter sweep.

A number of enemy aircraft were
destroyed on the ground, fixed installations were shot up, but no Japanese
aircraft were encountered in the air.

On 19th April the 15th and 21st
Groups teamed up once more on a
fighter sweep against Atsugi and
Yokosuka airfields. This time the
Japanese came up to intercept and in
the ensuing air battle Major James B
Tapp of the 15th Fighter Group became the first AAF ace over Japan by
destroying his fifth aircraft.

As leader of Blue Flight, Major Tapp
set up a patrol at 11,000 feet between
Yokohama and the Sagami River. The
flight patrolled until the squadron
leader called in to head for the rally
point. The flight headed for Sagami

A waist gunner's view of the escort

Bay and Major Tapp saw two Jack type fighters climbing from 8,000 feet. A flight of P-51s was attacking one of the Jacks so Major Tapp went after the other. A short burst sent the craft down in flames.

The air battles that day accounted for twenty-three enemy aircraft destroyed and the strafing attacks on the airfields accounted for another fourteen, with forty-three damaged. Two P-51s did not make it home.

Of particular importance on these long-range missions was the use of air/sea rescue methods. B-29s were used by the fighters as navigational and weather aircraft on the way to the target and return. The air/sea rescue B-29s were equipped to drop survival rafts and gear to ditched pilots, and submarines were posted at intervals on the routes of attack and return to pick up fighter pilots and bomber crews that had to go down in the water. So effective was this system that if a pilot or crew could get away from the Japanese main islands on the way home his chances of survival were very good.

The greatest single disaster to befall a formation of Mustangs occurred on the mission of 1st June, 1945. 148 P-51s of the 15th, 21st and 506th Fighter Groups took off on an escort mission to Osaka. When the fighters had reached a point approximately two hours away from home they entered a frontal area extending from the surface to 23,000 feet, where zero visibility, intense turbulence, heavy rain, snow and icy conditions scattered the P-51s so badly that it was impossible to maintain communiactions. Twenty-seven of the fighters broke out of the front and continued on to the target, and ninety-four returned to base. Twenty-four Mustangs were missing. Two of the pilots who bailed out in the front were later picked up by air/sea rescue vessels. No doubt many of the pilots became hopelessly lost in the 'Whiteout' conditions and flew blindly on until their fuel was exhausted.

Return to Iwo Jima after a busy day

By early summer 1945, the B-29s discontinued their high-altitude formation bombing and went to attacking their targets at night from medium to relatively low altitude. This largely ended the long range escort missions for the Mustangs. However, they continued to strike at enemy targets over Japan in their own fighter sweeps.

A sweep in the Tokyo area on 23rd June, 1945, was unusual in that air opposition was so intense that only one squadron of one of the groups was able to go down and strafe the airfield at Shimodate. More than sixty enemy fighters came up to engage and nine of them were shot down over the airfield. One P-51 was downed in the combat, with the pilot bailing out. This increase in enemy activity was no doubt due to the deep penetration of the Mustangs. Both primary targets were between 680 and 690 nautical miles from Iwo Jima by direct route and had not been hit before.

The total damage inflicted upon the Japanese on this fighter sweep was nineteen aircraft destroyed in the air and thirteen on the ground. Two Mustang pilots whose aircraft had been shot up on the mission managed to make it back to the rally point where they bailed out and were picked up by submarine.

On 10th August, 1945, Captain Abner M Aust was flying a Mustang on one of the last B-29 escort missions in the Tokyo area. The P-51 pilot was attacked by three Zekes, two of which he engaged in combat. One

of these he quickly shot down and the other fled after being hit.

Aust tangled with the third over Shiroi, but the anti-aircraft fire was so intense that both aircraft pulled up through the clouds which covered the airfield. When the Zeke popped up through the overcast Aust was ready for him. A long burst hit the Japanese aircraft full force; it shattered, burst into flames and crashed to earth.

When Aust returned to Iwo Jima he easily confirmed his first victory but no one had seen the second Zeke go down. This would have been his fifth victory and made him an ace. It would not be until 1959 when his brother-in-law was stationed in Japan and visited the sight of the crash would the victory be confirmed. There a wooden marker

Mount Fuji framed by the wings of B-29s

was found with the inscription 'In memoriam to a fallen Japanese aviator who met violent death on 10th August 1945'.

In August 1945, the dropping of the atomic bombs on Hiroshima and Nagasaki during that month brought the Second World War to a speedy close.

For the Mustang it was the end of a long war which had seen it meet with great success in all theaters of operations. While it won its fame primarily as a long-range escort fighter it had shown its excellence in every phase of operations in which it could possibly be utilised.

Epilogue

The North American P-51H, the ultimate Mustang, and probably the fastest piston-engined fighter to see service in the Second World War. The main distinguishing features were the smaller wheels, which allowed the leading edge extension of earlier models (to house the larger wheels) to be done away with, the slighter differently-shaped canopy and the taller vertical tail surfaces. The great improvement was the result of aerodynamic refinement, extreme weight saving in the structure and the great power of the superlative Merlin fitted. *Engine:* One Packard V-1650-9 Merlin inline, 2,218hp at 10,200 feet. *Armament:* Six Browning MG 53-2 .5-inch machine guns with 400 rounds (inner pair) and 270 rounds (outer two pairs) per gun or four .5-inch machine guns with 400 rounds per gun, plus two 500- or 1,000-lb bombs or six 5-inch rockets. *Speed:* 487mph at 25,000 feet. *Climb:* 5 minutes to 15,000 feet. *Ceiling:* 41,600 feet. *Range:* 755 miles clean and 1,530 miles maximum with two 63-gallon drop tanks. *Weight empty/loaded:* 6,585/11,500lbs. *Span:* 37 feet. *Length:* 33 feet 4 inches. *Role:* Long range fighter or fighter-bomber.

The end of the Second World War was by no means the end of the career of the North American P-51 Mustang. As a matter of fact, two production models of the aircraft came too late to see action in the conflict.

The lightweight P-51H was ordered in April of 1944 and flew in February of 1945. This aircraft was some 700lbs lighter than the P-51D and was fitted with the Packard V-1650-9 engine. This engine incorporated the Simmons boost control which made it possible to better maintain a preselected manifold pressure. A water injection system was also adapted to the engine for war emergency purposes. Through the use of water injection the engine was capable of developing more than 1,900 hp for a brief period of time.

Originally some 2,400 P-51Hs were ordered but the end of the war brought about drastic contract cancellations. The 550 P-51Hs that were built saw extensive duty with the Army Air Force and the Air National Guard in the postwar years.

Anticipating long range needs in the Pacific during the Second World War, the engineers at North American came up with the design for the P-82 Twin-Mustang. This aircraft was essentially two Mustang fuselages joined by a common center wing and horizontal stabiliser sections. The aircraft could carry a pilot in each cockpit or one cockpit could carry a navigator, depending on the mission requirements.

The long range configuration of the aircraft carried six .50 caliber machine guns in the center section of the wing and underwing racks were added to carry two 1,000-lb bombs. The outboard wing panels could be used for two additional 1,000-lb bombs or for droppable fuel tanks.

After the war the P-82 continued in production as a night fighter. A large radar pod was installed under the center wing section and the starboard cockpit was fitted with equipment for

The 'Twin Mustang' or P-82;

153

Another view of the P-82

a radar observer. The night fighter version of the P-82 was utilised into the mid-1950s.

When the Second World War aircraft were dumped on the war surplus market many Mustangs were purchased by sportsmen who wanted to modify the aircraft for air racing. When the cross country Bendix Race was reinaugurated in 1946 a Mustang flown by Paul Mantz took first place.

In 1947, Paul Mantz once more took first place in the California to Cleveland classic and the aircraft continued its dominance in 1948 with Mantz averaging 448 miles per hour in the highly modified Mustang.

Those Mustangs and Twin Mustangs which remained in the new United States Air Force were largely delegated to Alaska and the Pacific where they did yeoman duty during the late 1940s. In June of 1950 when South Korea was invaded it was an F-82 (formerly designated P-82) of the 68th All Weather Fighter Squadron that scored the first air to air victory.

Lieutenant William G Hudson was a member of a flight acting as top cover over Kimpo Airfield near Seoul, Korea, while American military dependents were being evacuated on 27th June, 1950. Five Russian built Yak fighters appeared and the Twin Mustangs destroyed three of them in the ensuing combat. The first of the three fell under the guns of Lieutenant Hudson.

The 8th, 35th and 49th Fighter-Bomber Groups all flew the Mustang during the early phases of the conflict in Korea while the 18th Fighter-Bomber Group operated in Mustangs until January of 1953. These USAF Mustangs were augmented by No 77 Squadron of the Royal Australian Air Force and No 2 Squadron of the South African Air Force. The Australians flew ground support in their Mustangs until April 1951 and the South Africans operated Mustangs

July 1951 – a Mustang lifts to attack communist ground installations

until January 1953.

Under the able leadership of Colonel Dean Hess, the Republic of South Korea Mustang unit grew from ten aircraft in 1950 to a full group of seventy-five P-51s. This unit flew many invaluable ground support missions with Hess taking part in over 250 of them.

The South Korean Air Force and a number of South and Central American countries continued to operate P-51s into the 1960s. The last active military Mustang in the United States was delivered to the Air Force Museum at Wright-Patterson AFB, Ohio, on 1st March, 1957.

Trans-Florida Aviation in Sarasota, Florida, was licensed by the Federal Aviation Administration to begin its remanufacture of Mustangs in February of 1959. This company began to turn out modified P-51s with the fuselage tank behind the pilot's seat removed and a 'buddy seat' installed. These sleek conversions especially adapted for sports flying were dubbed Cavaliers. Eventually the company adopted the name of Cavalier Aircraft and continued to turn out the reconditioned Mustangs not only for sports use but later as counter-insurgency aircraft for Central American countries. These latter modifications incorporated full armament systems and updated communications systems. The aircraft were furnished in limited quantity to Bolivia, the Dominican Republic, Guatemala and Salvador under the Military Assistance program.

The latest modification of the Mustang by Cavalier has been the Cavalier Mustang III which utilises the Rolls Royce Dart turbo-prop engine. Using this engine the aircraft has a dash speed of some 470 knots. Standard armament is six .50 caliber machine guns and provision is made to carry 110-gallon drop tanks for increased loiter time. This modification is still undergoing testing.

The era of the Mustang is far from over.

South Korean Air Force Mustangs
prepare to take off on a training
mission

Bibliography

Army Air Forces in World War II, volumes II & III, by W F Craven & J L Cate (eds) (University of Chicago Press)
Big Friend, Little Friend by Richard E Turner (Doubleday, New York)
Fighters Up by Erich Friedham and Samuel Taylor (MacCrae, New York)
Official Group and Squadron Histories (USAAF)
1000 Destroyed by Grover C Hall (Brown Printing Co, New York)
The Long Reach: VIII Fighter Command (USAAF)
The RCAF Overseas: The Fifth Year and *The Sixth Year* (Oxford University Press)
To the limit of their endurance: VIII Fighter Command (USAAF)